ROUTLEDGE LIBRARY EDITIONS:
COLD WAR SECURITY STUDIES

Volume 11

CHEMICAL WARFARE ARMS CONTROL

CHEMICAL WARFARE ARMS CONTROL

A Framework for Considering Policy Alternatives

JULIAN PERRY ROBINSON

Routledge
Taylor & Francis Group
LONDON AND NEW YORK

First published in 1985 by Taylor & Francis Ltd

This edition first published in 2021
by Routledge
2 Park Square, Milton Park, Abingdon, Oxon OX14 4RN

and by Routledge
605 Third Avenue, New York, NY 10017

Routledge is an imprint of the Taylor & Francis Group, an informa business

British Library Cataloguing in Publication Data
A catalogue record for this book is available from the British Library

ISBN: 978-0-367-56630-2 (Set)
ISBN: 978-0-367-62749-2 (Volume 11) (hbk)

Publisher's Note
The publisher has gone to great lengths to ensure the quality of this reprint but points out that some imperfections in the original copies may be apparent.

Disclaimer
The publisher has made every effort to trace copyright holders and would welcome correspondence from those they have been unable to trace.

Chemical Warfare Arms Control:

A framework for considering policy alternatives

by

Julian Perry Robinson

sipri

Stockholm International Peace Research Institute

Taylor & Francis
London and Philadelphia
1985

UK Taylor & Francis Ltd, 4 John Street, London WC1N 2ET
USA Taylor & Francis Inc., 242 Cherry Street, Philadelphia, PA 19106-1906

ISBN 0-85066-308-3
ISSN 0267-2537

ABSTRACT

Perry Robinson, Julian, Chemical Warfare Arms Control: A framework for considering policy alternatives. Taylor & Francis, London and Philadelphia, 1985, 116 pp. (Stockholm International Peace Research Institute). ISBN 0-85066-308-3.
This monograph focuses on the Geneva disarmament enterprise. What is attempted here is an overview: a way of thinking about chemical weapons from the standpoint of national policy-making in a manner that integrates both defence and arms-control aspects. No particular recommendations for policy are made, although the monograph is illustrated with examples of the sorts of conclusions that might be drawn from the analytical framework. Express attention is paid to some highly relevant considerations which the customs of diplomacy tend to push beneath the surface of intergovernmental discourse in Geneva--the influence of domestic interests and the need for a symbiotic relationship between national intelligence machinery and international verification machinery. The principal focus is on the core issue of verification.

Printed in Great Britain by Taylor & Francis (Printers) Ltd, Basingstoke, Hants.

Contents

Preface

Multilateral arms talks on chemical weapons have been proceeding in Geneva since 1968. They will still be doing so, most probably, in 1988. An optimist would expect that, by then, an international treaty would be in the very final stage of negotiation. That would be no small achievement, for actual negotiations did not formally begin until 1984. The previous 15 years had been given over to exploration of underlying issues and technical questions and to experiment with different forms of negotiating procedure. To the pessimist, and to the cynic, those are activities which could go on for another 15 years.

Yet the underlying issues and their associated technical questions are not simple, nor is the process of multilateral negotiation. It may be that, against their background of enormous and proliferating conventional and nuclear armament, chemical weapons do not really amount to much, suggesting that they could be got rid of without very much ado--certainly not 20 years of diplomatical discourse--if governments, and particularly the superpowers, so chose. The stakes would be far lower than for nuclear disarmament, so that chemical disarmament should be far the easier to achieve. Indeed, if the world could not agree on chemical weapons, how could it ever do so on weapons more heavily and widely relied upon by national armed forces? That, however, is only one side of the picture. If multilateral chemical arms control is to be effective, and if people and governments are to have lasting confidence in it, constraints will need to be placed on sectors of human activity far wider than appears at first glance. Chemistry, in its practical applications to human and social betterment, pervades vast expanses of scientific, manufacturing and economic endeavour, all of which are in principle adaptable rather easily to providing chemical weapons. Nuclear industry is, in contrast, minute. This has to mean, in effect, that governments can buy chemical disarmament only at significant political price. Reducing that price calls for great ingenuity and readiness to compromise from the negotiators.

Such is the underlying theme of the present monograph. It is written for people who are not necessarily specialists in either chemical warfare or in arms control but who nonetheless find themselves required to take a professional interest in chemical arms control: journalists, parliamentarians, officials newly assigned to the topic, and others in and around government engaged in research or study of public policy. Confronted by some aspect of chemical armament or of the Geneva chemical talks, it is easy for nonspecialists to become bemused by the surrounding technicalities and other details, and then to be either put off or misled. So what is attempted here is an overview: a portrayal of the problem of chemical disarmament in the round: a portrayal in which the component issues may be seen in clear relationship to one another and to wider aspects of national preparedness for the contingency of chemical warfare. This monograph therefore offers an analytical framework within which a wide spread of different considerations may be located and assessed: the factors which may cause any one particular proposal in the Geneva talks to appear, not only more or less attractive than some other proposal, but also more or less attractive than current national policies for chemical-warfare defence and deterrence.

This monograph, then, presents a way of thinking about chemical weapons from the standpoint of national policy-making. It is not meant to be anything more than this. It offers no particular recommendations for policy, although it is illustrated with examples of the sorts of conclusions that might be drawn from the analytical framework. It notes in passing a number of subsidiary topics on which more research seems to be needed before it would be worthwhile adding yet more proposals to the multitude which are already on the negotiating table in Geneva.

Publication of the monograph by SIPRI marks the start of a new series of SIPRI publications on chemical warfare that focus on the Geneva disarmament enterprise. The series will build upon and update its predecessor, **The Problem of Chemical and Biological Warfare**, which SIPRI began in 1967 and completed in 1975. The logic of inaugurating the new series with a conceptual study, rather than a prescriptive or purely descriptive one, and of publishing it now in occasional-paper rather than book format, is twofold. First, the number of people inside and outside government who are professionally engaged in chemical arms limitation, and who are thinking about its policy implications, has recently been growing rather rapidly. Perhaps the concepts which SIPRI is now in a position to put forward will assist newcomers to the field, even reduce the overall learning time. Second, the approach adopted in this monograph is bound to influence subsequent work in the SIPRI series. Its author is only too conscious of his limitations as an analyst of governmental behaviour and policy-making, and conscious, too, of the really expert nature of some of the work that has been done on the subject addressed, above all in and around the Conference on Disarmament in Geneva. The hope is that the criticism which this monograph may attract, and which SIPRI solicits keenly, will enable refinement of its analytical framework to the benefit of the series as a whole, thereby maximizing the contribution which SIPRI can make to the final extirpation of chemical warfare.

Specialists in the field will find that most of the ground covered in this monograph is familiar terrain. The approach is, however, a novel one in that it pays express attention to some highly relevant considerations which the customs of diplomacy tend to push beneath the surface of intergovernmental discourse in Geneva. Pre-eminent here are the ways in which domestic interests constrain negotiating positions, and the symbiosis which must ultimately exist between national intelligence machinery and international verification machinery. From the published record of the negotiations, it almost appears as though the prospects for agreement hinge entirely on the international relations of states, for those two crucial matters make no appearance there save either as conspicuous omission or when dissembled in exceptionally opaque euphemism. In exposing for consideration such domestic determinants of progress, it is hoped to make a wider audience more aware that chemical-warfare disarmament depends on factors much closer to home than those which are customarily thought of as directing international relations.

This approach finds its principal application in the core issue of verification. Here, too, what is said is rather different from what is usually said, chiefly because an approach has been sought which does not carry the mistrust-generating, and therefore counterproductive, implication that the chief purpose of the verification machinery is to discover or deter malefactors. The analysis proceeds instead from the premise (which is derived) that such machinery must be designed in order to promote assurance that each state party is, and will remain, better off inside the chemical-disarmament regime than outside it. The sort of question that is not asked, therefore, is: how should stockpile-destruction or nonproduction or nondiversion be verified? Instead, the question put is: why should such matters be verified--how, that is to say, would their verification promote assurance? From this may follow that guidance on two particular matters which has surely been missing for far too long: guidance on the proper targets, so to say, of the verification machinery--is it or is it not strictly necessary to verify this matter or that matter; and guidance on the stringency that should then be sought in each instance. Until such questions are answered, there is little purpose in reviewing all the technical possibilities for verification measures. That comes later.

The monograph is thus asking questions from first principles about the standards that are actually needed for verification. It looks in part for their definition at the interplay of domestic factors. It looks also at the security requirements, comparing the military means for satisfying them with various arms-control means, and differentiating degrees of chemical-warfare threat to see what each one may posit for assurance needs, and hence, in the arms-control route to security, for verification machinery. In this aspect, also, the monograph has a novelty which may be useful just now. Arms control is a specialized topic, so much so that it is far too often viewed apart from those other approaches to security, whether national or common, that are in the domain of the defence and strategic analysts. While options for arms-control policy may sometimes complement options for defence policy even to the extent that both may be taken up simultaneously, more often there is conflict between the two. In all areas of arms-control negotiation, then, there is need for some sort of common approach whereby the relative merits of competing military and arms-control options may be assessed according to common criteria. Im the particular field of chemical warfare, there have over the years been various studies of either the arms-control aspect or the defence aspect. With one especially notable exception [1], now somewhat dated, integrative studies have been almost entirely lacking. They are what are surely needed now if chemical arms control is to prosper against its present background of burgeoning attention to chemical rearmament. The analytical framework developed in this monograph is a contribution to this end; and the approach embodied in it may be found applicable in fields other than chemical warfare.

One consequence of the attempt to view the problem in the round is that it has revealed a number of topics that might guide possible solutions on which there is simply not enough information available. In part this is a consequence of the tightness with which governments, some far more so than others, hold the relevant data. But in part, too, it reflects failure by the research community to recognize needs for additional inquiry. With a view to stimulating further research, the more important of these topics are identified in the text as they occur.

The flow of argument in this monograph is its main point. So as not to interrupt it, much of the substantiating technical and historical detail has been excluded from the text. It will be published later in the series, principally in <u>Chemical and Biological Warfare Data Book</u>.

Readers unfamiliar with the subject of chemical warfare may find an inconvenient lack of background information in this monograph, especially historical information. For that they may be referred to earlier SIPRI publications (listed on the inside back cover), especially volumes 1 and 4 of The Problem of Chemical and Biological Warfare and the reviews published in the 1982, 1983, 1984 and 1985 SIPRI Yearbooks. There are five items of chemical-warfare history of which it is as well, in this introduction, to remind readers:

Poison gas was first used on a large scale during World War I, causing well over a million casualties.

Poison gas has never been used on a comparable scale since, not even during World War II when the total quantities stockpiled, by all the major belligerents, were probably well over quarter of a million tons, easily double that which was consumed during World War I.

Poison gas has, however, been used on a relatively small scale in several wars since 1918, all of them in underdeveloped regions of the world, though probably in a far smaller number of wars than contemporary allegations suggest. The most recent episode has been in the present Iraq-Iran war.

Chemical weapons in the form, not of poison gas, but of chemical herbicides and tear gases, were used on a large scale during the Viet Nam War, especially during 1965-70, the total tonnage of toxic chemicals disseminated then approaching that of World War I.

Draft chemical disarmament treaties have been put forward during the period of the current negotiations on chemical arms limitation in Geneva by the USSR jointly with her principal allies in 1972 [2], by the group of nonaligned countries in 1973 (an outline draft) [3], by Japan in 1974 [4], by Britain in 1976 [5], and by the USA in 1984 [6]. In 1980, the USA and the USSR tabled the last of a series of joint documents reporting the consensus they had registered during an inconclusive series of private bilateral talks on chemical disarmament that had begun in 1976 [7].

The following abbreviations are used in this monograph:

BW	Biological warfare
BWC	The 1972 Biological and Toxin Weapons Convention
CBW	Chemical and biological warfare
CCD	The Conference of the Committee on Disarmament
CD	The Committee on Disarmament, or, since 1984, the Conference on Disarmament
CW	Chemical warfare
CWC	The projected Chemical Weapons Convention
ENDC	The Eighteen-Nation Disarmament Committee

Chapter 1. The purpose of the Geneva negotiations

Origins

We can begin in Geneva, in the summer of 1968. That was when the governments represented on the old Eighteen Nation Disarmament Committee, the ENDC, agreed to admit the topic of chemical and biological warfare onto their agenda. It was this decision, taken under the co-chairmanship of the USA and the USSR in furtherance of a proposal by Sweden, which set the Geneva talks onto the course which we see today: a course which led surprisingly quickly to the 1972 Biological and Toxin Weapons Convention and, by Article IX of that treaty, locked governments into negotiation on a Chemical Weapons Convention.

Why the participating governments took that decision can no doubt be explained in several ways. Some interpretations might look to the political environment of the Viet Nam War, then at the forefront of international attention. Increasing resort to toxic chemicals--in fact herbicides and tear gases--as weapons was a feature of that war, an aspect on which the anti-war movement in the United States and elsewhere had focused, and to which Hungary had, in the autumn of 1966, formally directed the attention of the United Nations General Assembly. The international community also had before it reports of poison-gas warfare from the civil war in what was then the Yemen. Other explanations might also look to the influence of the incipient SALT process, and to the growing political strength of environmentalist movements in some countries at that time. Still others might give importance to the calls from within the international community for progress--any progress--towards the goal of general and complete disarmament which the ENDC had been established six years earlier to promote. All accounts would have to note the peculiar horror which poison-gas and germ warfare are capable of arousing, and the professional disdain towards CBW weapons which military people often display.

Whatever it was that really set things going in Geneva, however, there was one contributory factor which, since then, has continued to stimulate the enterprise: a widespread sense that the existing regime of international law and custom which constrained resort to CBW was under mounting threat, and that it might well prove to be in the best interests of all states if that regime were somehow to be strengthened. The cornerstone, though by no means the sole element, of the anti-CBW regime was an international treaty then nearly half a century old: the Protocol for the Prohibition of the Use in War of Asphyxiating, Poisonous or Other Gases, and of Bacteriological Methods of Warfare, signed at Geneva on 17 June 1925. With two important exceptions, all leading states were then parties. The exceptions were Japan, which joined the treaty in 1970, and the United States, which joined in 1975.

Motivations, objectives and interest groups

Seventeen years on from that ENDC decision, we can scarcely fail to recognize from the ups and downs of the ensuing talks that the motivations which direct the stances of the participating delegations are varied, given to change, and not necessarily in full harmony with declared objectives. Though this may be a matter for concern, it can hardly be one for surprise. The delegations are representative of governments which themselves represent a more or less continual realignment of domestic interests--a changing ascendancy of different factions, some standing to gain, others to lose, from one or another turn of events. That is so for all governments, whatever their complexion--capitalist, socialist or any other. Progress towards the projected Chemical Weapons Convention is bound to be paced as much, perhaps far more, by accommodations being reached within governments as by negotiations between them. Perhaps it is because the application of arms control to CW could affect, positively and negatively, so many interests--industrial, military, scientific and bureaucratic, all of them of several kinds and often inter-related--that the talks have been so long in coming either to fruition or to collapse. The framework of analysis which we are seeking must adequately display these domestic factors, especially as they affect the major parties to the negotiation. Indeed, this seems so important that it is on a concept of advantaged and disadvantaged interest-groups that we shall build framework.

What happens in Geneva may indeed often be no more than a reflection or shadow of what is happening in the major capitals, and to that extent detailed analysis of the actual issues engaging the Geneva delegations may not have much that is useful to teach about alternative ways forward. Yet it would be wrong to see the proceedings of the ENDC and its successor bodies--the CCD and now the CD--solely as shadow-play. In the record of their work on CW, there is now a long register of intergovernmental consensus reached on ideas initially generated in Geneva. While it is true that there is also a lengthy record of other such ideas apparently having been trampled upon, and thus lost from sight, in clashes of opinion in the major capitals, there remain signs that the CD has now acquired enough authority on CW matters for its proceedings to exert a direct influence on the policy-making of some, if not all, of the governments represented by its 40 members. That influence may not always be strong; and its effect may be no more than to set more or less loose bounds to the freedom of bureaucratic and other domestic interests to dictate national negotiating positions. Of course, if there were no such influence at all, the CD would be a charade: an embodiment of precisely that for which its critics deride it, namely the futility of multilateral negotiation as an instrument of worthwhile arms control, let alone as a route to disarmament.

Having joined in negotiation, the participating governments have formally and publicly committed themselves to principles which have since been directing the work of the CD on chemical warfare. And as that work has advanced, so too has a record accumulated of positions taken and views expressed by individual governments: stances towards particular issues which are bound to condition those that could be adopted in the future. These are the circumstances which enable the CD to exert its limiting influence, such as it is, on the opposing pressures generated within national decision-making processes by affronted interests. There are bound, for example, to be sectors of conservative opinion in all countries that see additional arms control as inimical to their ideas of prudent force-planning for the protection of the national security. There will be industrial interests in centrally planned no less than market economies that perceive threats to their well-being in any controls on manufacturing activity. Within the armed services and their associated defence bureaucracies, there will be elements that see the negotiations as endangering their status and their institutions, especially in countries that have active chemical-weapons programmes. Scientific interests can be expected to resist limits to their freedom of inquiry or communication. From some or all of them, an effective Chemical Weapons Convention may demand sacrifices. The CD's directing principles, embodied within the mandate given to the CD by the governments represented on it and endorsed by the General Assembly of the United Nations, in effect declare the existence of a greater good to which factional interests must be subordinated.

That may be; but idealists rarely command much strength in governmental or bureaucratic politics. So it is apparent that, if the negotiations are to succeed, they can do so only if the sacrifices are kept to the barest minimum still consonant with a worthwhile goal. Here, then, is the first question that must be resolved in our analysis: what, realistically, might that goal be?

Weaknesses in the existing anti-CW regime

We may loosely define the goal in the terms already stated: a Chemical Weapons Convention that will somehow strengthen the international regime symbolized by the 1925 Geneva Protocol. That treaty prohibits the "use in war of asphyxiating, poisonous or other gases, and of all analogous liquids, materials or devices". But other than this very generally and, on certain points, ambiguously worded rule, the treaty makes little in the way of substantive provision. Neither it nor any of the other conventional international law establishing the regime lays down procedures whereby states parties may seek to resolve disputes about implementation of the rule or compliance with it; nor are mechanisms provided for states parties to arrive at collective decisions on such matters. Any such actions would probably require the convening of a special conference of states parties to the Geneva Protocol; which, since there are now about 120 of them, would be a most cumbersome and difficult proceeding, very probably imparting a political moment out of all proportion to the end sought, and therefore counterproductive to it. In short, the regime associated with the Geneva Protocol is a tenuous one. It is true that there is now the evidence of several UN General Assembly resolutions to indicate that the treaty may by now be achieving its declared objective. Its prohibition of chemical warfare (and the extension of that prohibition to biological warfare) may indeed be becoming "universally accepted as a part of International Law, binding alike the conscience and the practice of nations". Yet that objective has as its safeguard no more than a collection of signatures testifying merely to the existence, at the moment of their execution and any subsequent ratification or reaffirmation, of a certain collective state of mind eschewing intention of ever resorting to CBW. Intentions may not persist unless they are somehow locked into place. We may conclude, then, that there is ample room for strengthening the regime and that, at least to this extent, the present Geneva negotiations have a reasonable objective.

We can say, further, that this objective is also a timely one. If the fears of 1968 that the existing consensus of states against CBW was beginning to fall apart--that intentions were fading--were justified then, they are still more justified now. Over the past ten years there have been reports of the use of CBW weapons in at least 16 different conflicts. Close inquiry would probably show that the incidence of alleged resorts to CBW has been increasing at a rate faster than that of the incidence of wars. Many of the reports are no doubt false or mistaken, reflecting the high emotiveness of CBW and the readiness with which that characteristic lends itself to propaganda purposes. But probably not all of them are false. In March 1984, the UN Secretary-General provided what was essentially conclusive verification that CW had occurred earlier that month in the Iraq-Iran war, whose belligerents are long-standing parties to the Geneva Protocol. Others of the reports have not received that degree of impartial verification, but some of them, notably those from Afghanistan during 1979-83 and those associated with the 'yellow rain' episodes in southeast Asia, have attracted a sufficiently influential range of believers to threaten general confidence in the regime. Mutual confidence among states parties is all that sustains the regime, and may be damaged by mistaken suppositions of noncompliance as well as by correct ones. For as long as the regime lacks procedures for differentiating the true from the false it is bound to be more precarious than it could otherwise be. A strengthening of the regime at least to the extent of establishing such procedures may thus be seen as an urgent objective.

Is the regime worth strengthening?

There is, however, a contrary consideration. One interpretation of the growing number of reports of chemical warfare may indeed be that the regime is weakening and needs to be strengthened. But another interpretation is that the regime is actually irrelevant, and perhaps always has been, save as a device which governments may use to strike attitudes upon the international stage, and domestically too: that the regime exerts no practical influence upon wartime behaviour and the choice of weapons. Such an interpretation would explain the relative rarity of chemical-weapons employment during earlier decades and especially during World War II, not in terms of a general desire to comply with the relevant international law, but in terms of the generally low military utility of chemical weapons. If use of the weapons is in fact now increasing, that is because the nature of armed conflict has been changing and, with it, the usefulness of chemical warfare. If there is truth in this explanation, why then should yet another collection of governmental signatures by laborious treaty negotiation in Geneva be in any way worthwhile? Why bother to strengthen a regime which, on this line of reasoning, may be mere make-believe?

Whether the Geneva Protocol has or has not inhibited resort to chemical warfare is accordingly an important topic for historical researach. The evidence that has thus far been discerned upon inquiry in state archives is that the Protocol has indeed had an inhibitory effect, but not so much as a constraint on the behaviour of belligerents in time of war as on their prior peacetime behaviour. The record suggests that the Protocol has damped the prosecution of CW armament programmes that might otherwise have provided belligerents with attractive military options after war had broken out. The Geneva Protocol has, in other words, retarded the assimilation of chemical weapons into the forces and the military doctrines of states [8, 9]; a matter to which we shall return in chapter 4. Weapons that are poorly assimilated are, ipso facto, incapable of being used to the full extent of their inherent utility. While it may be true that the common abstention from chemical warfare over the past six decades has, as the contrary explanation proposes, been due primarily to the low military usefulness of chemical weapons, that in itself has been a partial consequence of the Geneva Protocol. The available evidence in support of this assessment of the Protocol is by no means conclusive, and will remain inconclusive for as long as the national archives of such major states as the USSR and France remain unexplored. But the fact that there is any supporting evidence at all is a sufficient conclusion for our present purposes.

The question of the military utility of CW raises a further and less academic issue. If--for whatever reason--the military value of chemical weapons is slight, then why should an international regime be needed any longer to prevent their use? If, conversely, their military value is significant, that will in any case demand that allowance be made for them, as for any other category of weapon, in national defence planning; and why make the task of the planners any more complicated by imposing upon their work the uncertainties that are bound to flow from an international regime operating within a changing international environment? Either way, is there really anything about chemical weapons that makes them a special case for treatment by negotiators in Geneva?

This question may be considered from a variety of standpoints, ethical ones not least. An affirmative answer would imply that, for the national policy on chemical weapons which a state should follow, collaboration in the international regime which the negotiations could create would be an option altogether better than purely national measures of self-reliance--reliance on special forms of defence, deterrence or related military measures. The implication would be, in other words, that there was something so peculiar in the nature of CW armament--something not displayed by other forms of armament--as positively to militate against its exploitation in the service of the national defence and in favour of international collaboration against it. Two factors above all suggest that this is indeed so.

One factor is that a degree of collaboration already exists in the Geneva-Protocol-based regime. This regime has, moreover, been significantly extended in recent years by the entries into force of the 1972 Biological Weapons Convention (which bans the development, production and stockpiling of, amongst other things, some types of toxic weapons, namely 'toxins') in 1975, and the 1977 Environmental Modification Convention (which places new restrictions on herbicide warfare) in 1980. This means that, as regards chemical weaopns, defence planners are constrained even now by extraneous international factors in their choice of options for national self-reliance. Above all, the planners are formally precluded from allowing their forces the initiative in using chemical weapons, even for the territorial defence of the homeland. Either this constraint is ignored, in which case a whole range of political costs are liable to be incurred nationally and internationally if and when the fact of the disregard for treaty-commitments becomes apparent outside the defence-planning community. Or the constraint is accepted, in which case chemical weapons assume the character solely of menace, being instruments to which resort may be made solely on the initiative of enemies. Chemical weapons, with biological weapons, are unique in this awkward, outcaste and threatening status.

The second factor follows in part from the first. At least as regards the leading Western and nonaligned countries, in all of which it is demonstrably the case that the Geneva Protocol regime has retarded assimilation of chemical weapons, it may be assumed that the available technology of chemical weaponry falls short of that which, in the absence of constraint, the applicable science could otherwise provide. For all that can be judged from open sources, the same could be true for the leading Eastern countries, too. The applicable science is, moreover, fast developing into new areas of knowledge, as in the field of recombinant DNA research, from which yet more novel CBW weapon concepts might be drawn. Alongside all of this, structural change is happening within the chemical and allied manufacturing industries, typified by current investment in biotechnologies, change that might facilitate the large-scale entry of new CBW weapon-concepts into the arsenals. There may accordingly exist major potential for rapid transformation of the present lowly status of CBW weapons within national force-structures: the potential, in short, for a dramatic, and therefore stability-endangering, new arms race. It would, moreover, be an arms race of potentially enormous social cost, for it would inevitably deform the sciences and the technologies that sustained it, weakening their responsiveness to social needs. In view of the sheer extent of all this uncharted terrain, one might doubt whether even a superpower could enter such a race with any reasonable expectation of gaining advantage or diminishing disadvantage thereby: a clear argument, one might then suppose, in favour of measures of international collaboration designed to protect states from being sucked willy-nilly into such dangerous competition.

International collaboration and national sovereignty

This is not the place to discuss the several other considerations which justify the special treatment that chemical weapons are receiving in Geneva. For present purposes the important thing to note is this: by endorsing the goal of a strengthened anti-CW regime, the governments represented on the CD are in effect stating their preference for international collaboration over self-reliance as a means for coping with CW, for it is that preference which underlies--is in fact the central characteristic of--any international regime. By continuing to negotiate, governments are reaffirming that preference, which we may now see as the most important of the CD's directing principles referred to earlier.

Where there remains room for doubt about the realism of the goal is in a central implication of the preference. Co-operation in an international regime whose intended effect is to constrain certain aspects of potential state behaviour necessarily requires some diminution of the national sovereignty of the collaborants. If it did not, the constraints would either be unnecessary or ineffective. Most states today are enmeshed in so many networks of economic, military and other collaboration, some of which bear heavily upon their security, that any additional limits to their sovereign freedom imposed by a strengthened anti-CW regime might seem a small price to pay for the benefits that could result. Yet there may be other states, ones which would presumably thereby be declaring themselves more self-reliant, for whom such diminution might be far less tolerable, requiring major and immediate compensating benefit even to be thinkable. The question then is whether the benefits to be drawn from a strengthened anti-CW regime could in fact ever be great enough in the perceptions of such states to allow their co-operation in the creation of the regime. If not, the Geneva negotiations are pointless and the postulated objective unattainable.

An outline framework of analysis

Our initial scrutiny of the Geneva goal has thus displayed for further attention a number of preliminary conclusions, new questions, and ways of conceiving the underlying problems. We may use all this to build the beginnings of a framework of analysis within which the Geneva negotiating options may be seen in clearer relation to one another and to other CW policy options.

The outline framework classifies the alternatives facing states for their future policies on CW into two broad categories. In one category are policies of co-operation with some form of international regime whose structure remains open for negotiation. In the other category are policies of national self-reliance whose execution will remain primarily with the military. The categories are not necessarily mutually exclusive. Although in some areas measures of national self-reliance may conflict with the requirements of an effective international regime and would, if pursued, destroy the regime, in other areas such measures may be seen as positively enhancing the regime by diminishing the risks of subordination to it. Associated with each of the varied subsidiary options for policy in either category is a set of costs and benefits. The goal of the negotiations is to design a regime in which the balance of benefit is such as to favour the collaboration of all participants, and to offer greater overall benefit than policies of self-reliance alone.

In the design of the regime, the negotiators have three sets of variables that can be adjusted so as to alter the balance of cost and benefit, the variables corresponding to the principal elements of any international regime [10, 11]. There is, first, the set of norms encapsulating the common purpose of the regime. The basic norm in the present anti-CW regime is the consensus expressed in the preamble of the Geneva Protocol: agreement that resort to CW is and always will be contrary to civilized behaviour, a shared attitude whose preservation is the purpose of the Protocol. Second, there is a set of procedures which participants in the regime agree to adopt to ensure implementation of its purpose. The present anti-CW regime is remarkable, as we have noted, for its absence of any such procedures: prescribed courses of action, for example, which states parties should follow in the event of appearances of noncompliance, appearances that might otherwise lead participants to withdraw their collaboration in the regime. Finally, there is a set of <u>rules</u> mediating between the purpose of the regime and its implementation. The present anti-CW regime has, in effect, only one formal rule, which is essentially a restatement of its purpose: chemical weapons shall not be used in war.

In order to facilitate implementation, the draftsmen of the Geneva Protocol might perhaps have formulated additional rules whose function would have been to prevent divisive disputes about, for example, what was or was not a 'chemical weapon'. That, in this instance, they chose not to has had a beneficial consequence which warrants special note here. Had such additional rules been provided, they might well have had the effect of locking the treaty into the technology and attitudes of the 1920s. By keeping the rules to a minimum, the draftsmen safeguarded the forward-looking character of the Protocol, ensuring the relevance of the regime in the decades ahead. Simplicity thus proved to be a virtue.

This outline framework of analysis is applicable to the basic question formulated above: what objective may realistically be expected of the Geneva CW negotiations having due regard to the interests at stake? Such an application, which we begin in the next chapter, will allow us to develop the framework further.

Chapter 2. The scope of the projected Chemical Weapons Convention

Formulating a new norm of international behaviour

What may be inferred from our analysis thus far about the norms of international behaviour which should find expression in the projected Chemical Weapons Convention and which are to establish the purpose of the anti-CW regime as strengthened by the new treaty? What, in other words, should be the scope of the treaty that is to be negotiated?

We have seen that the principal norm defining the present anti-CW regime is abstention from chemical warfare, the purpose of the regime thus being to prevent any recurrence of chemical warfare, a purpose which it seeks to effect by requiring compliance with a rule of international law prohibiting chemical warfare. In comparison with other international regimes in existence today--on atomic energy, for example, or narcotic drugs--the anti-CW regime is a primitive one. Even so, may its underpinning norm still be a sufficient one for the projected Chemical Weapons Convention, or must consensus be sought around something more ambitious? If the norm is sufficient, then the objective of the Geneva negotiations need be no more than to secure agreement on additional rules and procedures, such as those already suggested, whose effect would be to provide greater assurance of compliance with the regime. If a more ambitious norm is needed, then what may be said about the maximal and minimal bounds within which the new consensus should be reached?

Why a norm only of non-use is insufficient

The Geneva negotiators have, in effect, long since agreed that the present norm is insufficient for their purposes. We can see that this is because the norm is also inadequate for the purpose of the existing anti-CW regime, for the scope of the rules which would be required to implement that purpose fully is broader than the embrace of the norm. In other words, a new norm must be found from within which rules of law may be derived which, if complied with fully, will necessarily preclude resort to chemical warfare. It might be supposed that the existing rule, which is to say the prohibition enunciated by the Geneva Protocol, is actually sufficient for this purpose. But it is not, for three reasons.

First, the laws of war of which the Geneva Protocol is a part include the device of belligerent reprisals as a sanction lending force to the law. In essence, this device condones otherwise illegal acts of war when their intention is to halt a continuing violation of the laws of war by the opposing belligerent. On the occasion of the first widely publicized violation of the Geneva Protocol, it was as an act of belligerent reprisal that Italy sought to justify the use of chemical weapons which she had begun in Ethiopia during 1935, adducing evidence of Ethiopian atrocities.

Second, the rule is stated as a contract between the parties to the Protocol. Should the contract be broken by Country A at war with Country B, then B would be freed from her obligations and might legitimately resort to chemical warfare without limiting its scale and duration to that of belligerent reprisal. Nor would it necessarily have had to have been the case that Country A in fact made the resort to CW which precipitated B's response. In the absence of prescribed procedures for ascertaining noncompliance with the rule, Country B might have been acting on a mistaken or even a contrived supposition. And if either A or B were not a party to the Protocol, the rule would in any case not apply. Japan, not then a party to the Geneva Protocol, evidently considered herself free to use chemical weapons in China during 1937-42. While it is true that the purely contractual nature of the Geneva-Protocol rule is now disputed by wide sectors of juridical opinion, it being commonly maintained that the rule has now become binding upon all states whether they are or are not parties to the Protocol, this view of the prohibition of

CW now having become a rule of customary international law is apparently not shared by all governments. The British government, for example, like the French, does not share such a view. Nor, until rather recently, did the US government. The stance of the Soviet government has been ambivalent: sometimes it has appeared to subscribe to the view, but at other times not. Until there is unanimity of opinion on the matter, the question of whether the customary rule is binding even upon states that have been attacked with chemical weapons must remain moot.

Third, although the rule is arguably an absolute ban on chemical warfare, it is in fact interpreted by many influential governments as a no-first-use agreement, one that permits resort to chemical warfare as retaliation in kind. The right to execute such retaliation was expressly reserved by 34 governments when ratifying or acceding to the Geneva Protocol, including those of France, the USSR, Britain, China and the USA, although not that of Germany. Whether to give substance to such reservations or for quite other reasons, countries might consider it prudent to acquire and maintain stocks of chemical weapons--actions which, subject to certain not especially limiting restrictions and with the exception of a small number of countries, they are at present perfectly entitled to take. Several countries did so after the time that they became bound by the Geneva Protocol, most of them under the stimulus of World War II when there were at least 12 possessor states. A few, including France, the USA and the USSR, are known to maintain stocks today, and others in increasing number are alleged to do so.

Need for a norm of nonpossession

We can thus see that the norm of abstention from CW has not been, nor could it ever be, guaranteed by a rule which simply restates that norm as a prohibition in international law. Such a rule can operate only by positively legitimizing forms of chemical warfare which it is necessarily incapable of prohibiting, namely the use of chemical weapons in reprisal and perhaps retaliation in kind. Such legitimation may possibly have the effect, through deterrence, of enforcing the rule, in which case the rule might take on the appearance of effectiveness and the purpose of the regime be fulfilled. That would, however, be an achievement, not of the international regime that had provided the rule, but of the national measures of self-reliance that had provided the deterrence. Since those self-same measures could also provide the means for violating the rule, and since it is by no means clear that chemical weapons per se are in fact capable of deterring resort to chemical warfare--any more than guns can necessarily deter resort to conventional warfare--we can see that that rule alone is not enough. It is obvious that confidence in the purpose of the regime actually being implemented--sufficient confidence for national measures of self-reliance to be relaxed--requires additional rules that prohibit possession of chemical weapons.

But the norm embodied in the present regime provides no mandate for the development of such additional rules. Here, then, is the minimum bound for the range within which consensus must needs be sought on a new international norm. If chemical warfare is to be prevented by international agreement, the nations of the world must forswear chemical weapons. The new norm must at least be that possession of chemical weapons is and always will be contrary to civilized behaviour, and repugnant to the conscience of mankind: this must be among the attitudes that all states parties to the projected Chemical Weapons Convention declare that they share and which it will be a function of the treaty to preserve. Such an objective for the Geneva negotiations has long been accepted in principle. The only substantial disagreements in practice relate to the detail of what is or is not to be regarded as a chemical weapon, a matter taken up in chapter 6.

Partial measures

We should note that in accepting this disarmament objective, the negotiators have rejected certain lesser objectives which might not be without value if achieved and implemented. It is worth identifying some of them here, for if the negotiations run into serious difficulties they could perhaps provide an acceptable fallback objective.

Nonpossession undertakings within qualitative limits can and have been envisaged. For example, when bilateral US-Soviet contacts on chemical weapons began in 1974, the initial communique referred to "the most dangerous, lethal means" of chemical warfare, implying the possibility of a ban on nerve-gas weapons only. A rationale for so narrow a scope is provided by the concept of 'weapons of mass destruction', a concept which has underlain the disarmament philosophy of the United Nations since its inception. But such an approach was sharply criticized on the grounds that it would discriminate against states for which chemical weapons of, say, World War I vintage (the pre nerve-gas era) might represent a serious menace. Comprehensiveness of scope thereafter became the declared objective, and remains so today, though it now looks doubtful whether it will entirely survive the controversy over what is and is not to be considered a chemical weapon.

Another type of qualitative limitation that is at least conceivable is one that parallels the widely argued view that the current prohibition of CW in international law amounts to no more than a ban on the first use of chemical weapons. Might it be possible to negotiate a regime whose function would merely be to reduce the possibilities whereby retaliatory stocks of chemical weapons could be used to initiate chemical warfare? Such an objective would be fully in keeping with the tenets of arms-control theory as it has developed in the West since the late 1950s. In view not least of the positive incentive it would create for countries to embark upon chemical armament programmes, it is fortunate that such a path has been rejected. It is, in any case, almost certainly impracticable.

Nonpossession norms operating at least initially within limited geographical regions have also been contemplated: the establishment of a chemical-weapons-free zone within the Tlatelolco Treaty area, for example, or central Europe. The latter was the subject of talks at party-political level--SED and SPD--which began between the two German states early in 1984. It is seen by its advocates as a stepping-stone or stimulus to a worldwide nonpossession agreement, and by its detractors as an obstacle to, or at least a diversion from, that wider objective. The practical value of zone concepts must ultimately rest on whether a regional regime could serve a purpose that would remain useful even with the nonparticipation of those contiguous countries wherein the balance of domestic power evidently precluded effective implementation of a global regime.

Adequacy of a nonpossession norm: intentions, capability and warning time

States that do not possess chemical weapons cannot use them: to this extent, compliance with a global nonpossession norm would prevent the recurrence of chemical warfare. Whether such a norm would, for that reason, be sufficient turns on the question of confidence. Many chemical weapons are not especially difficult to make, so that a country determined to use them could acquire stocks within a relatively short period after deciding to abrogate a nonpossession undertaking. The lag-time might be short enough to deny other countries sufficient warning of the need to take countermeasures. Considered in security terms, therefore, the overall benefit to states from their collaboration in a nonpossession regime might reasonably be judged far too slight for policies of national self-reliance to be relaxed to the point of compatibility with the regime. The remedy would then be to seek a regime that would afford a longer warning time of any impending security-threatening abrogation. This could be achieved by some or all of several conceivable measures which would retard the processes either (a) of acquiring supplies of chemical weapons sufficient to pose a threat, or (b) of bringing the forces that would use those supplies to a state of readiness sufficient to execute the threat. The desirable norm would not then be one only of nonpossession; it would be a norm forswearing activities that could facilitate resort to chemical warfare.

There is, in theory, a wide range of different activities which may reasonably be regarded as falling within such a category. The more that are included, the wider would be the range of interests likely to be associated with their continuation, and therefore the more difficult the task of reaching consensus on their limitation. Here, in table 1 below, is a representative list, all of its items being taken from working papers tabled by national delegations during the Geneva negotiations:

Table 1. Activities that could facilitate resort to chemical warfare

(a) As regards supplies of CW agents or devices for using them	(b) As regards readiness to use such supplies
Retention	Planning
Stockpiling	Organizing
Deployment on the territories of other countries	Disseminating requisite information
Production	Training
Other acquisition	Practising
Transfer	Conducting other activities in preparation for use other than any of those listed above
Trading	
Transfer of know-how for acquiring	
Transfer of key materials for acquiring	
Developing	
Testing	
Research aimed at production	
Assisting, encouraging, permitting or inducing any of the foregoing by other states or international organizations, directly or indirectly	

The full magnitude of the potential conflicts of interest becomes apparent when it is appreciated that the activities listed under (a) of table 1 may all include activities involving chemicals that have peaceful as well as CW applications (directly, as poisons, or indirectly, as manufacturing intermediates for poisons), the so-called 'dual-purpose chemicals', and that activities listed under (b) would inevitably overlap strongly upon normal military pursuits serving requirements that have nothing whatever to do with use of chemical weapons. It might therefore be concluded that consensus on even a small fraction of the listed activities would be unattainable: that, as between the maximal and minimal bounds represented by the listing within which agreement is to be sought on the norm that is to underpin the CWC, only one that is located close to the minimum bound could offer a goal that is at all realistic.

That, however, would be to mistake the purpose of the norm for the purpose of the treaty. If it is accepted that the obstructions that would otherwise be created by affronted domestic interests require that the CWC be designed to serve no further practical purpose than strengthening the existing anti-CW regime, then the maximal function of the CWC is no more than to preclude chemical warfare by banning chemical weapons. It cannot be the function of the CWC to outlaw, for example, all research that could be put to use in the production of chemical weapons, or any international exchange of information that could facilitate use of chemical weapons. Outright bans on these or on any of the other activities listed in table 1 would be required only to the extent that without such rules states parties would be denied the confidence they would need in the regime as a whole. The purpose of the norm is to provide the mandate for the derivation of reassuring rules: rules that may be codified in the CWC itself or by any amending actions during the subsequent lifetime of the CWC. The norm need therefore take the form only of a collective expression of willingness to forswear all activities intended to facilitate resort to chemical warfare.

The consensus of governments on a norm couched in this fashion should present no great problems. Both the USSR and the USA have already put forward forms of wording consonant with it: "The world's peoples are demanding that ... the very possibility of the use of chemical weapons should be ruled out" [12]; and "Determined, for the sake of all mankind, to exclude completely the possibility of toxic chemicals being used as weapons" [6].

With agreement on a norm of such extensive scope, the goal of the Geneva negotiations then becomes consensus on a set of derived rules and procedures giving states enough confidence in the continuing preclusion of security-threatening chemical warfare for them to relax, or forgo adopting, measures of national self-reliance against that menace which are incompatible with the regime thereby created. The set of rules and procedures need provide no more, and must provide no less, assurance than this that the declarations of intention embodied in the norm remain valid.

A fuller framework of analysis

A logic for specifying the desirable scope of the CWC is thus apparent. We can use it to develop further the framework of analysis outlined at the end of chapter 1.

Let us build upon the simple cost-benefit structure of the framework by visualizing the process whereby a state selects its CW policies as a process of barter between the two broad options of international collaboration and national self-reliance. On the one side of the deal there is the international regime that is to be created by the CWC, the exact provisions of which remain to be determined, but whose function is to ban chemical weapons. The state will have opportunity through its diplomacy, some states more effectively than others, to influence the form of the regime so as to align its provisions with national needs. These needs are defined by the prevailing balance of domestic interests. How far that alignment can go will of course be limited by the available scope for intergovernmental compromise. On the other side of the barter, there is the range of military and related options specifiable for safeguarding the state against the menace of adversary CW. Again, what the state decides it needs is determined by the prevailing balance of domestic power among groups holding different opinions. Some of these options may already have been implemented. Others, or even all of them, may have been left open. A few of the options would be incompatible with a ban on chemical weapons and would therefore, under the terms of the CWC, have to be forgone.

The barter may thus be seen as a deal in which a basket of military options (open or already implemented) is traded for a basket of regime undertakings. Basket-value is set by what each basket both includes and excludes. The content that would make the regime-basket more valuable than the military basket would determine the state's negotiating objective in Geneva. If intergovernmental agreement on it does not prove possible, things may eventually have to be transferred from one basket to the other, or new things put into one or the other, in order to keep the negotiations alive. But this could endanger the domestic consensus by requiring sacrifices from influential interests. The Geneva negotiations, then, proceed through a process in which the intergovernmental negotiators seek to reconcile the different national outcomes of intragovernmental negotiations that have sought concessions from those disaffected domestic interests that command influence upon governmental policy.

This conception compels our attention to its two chief elements. First, what precisely are the different items that might be placed in each basket or withheld from them? Second, what may be the measure of value with which the worth of one basket is assessable against the worth of the other? These are matters that will be addressed in later chapters. Let us first note the illumination which our barter analogy provides of the core problem confronting the Geneva negotiators. It is this: the international-collaboration basket, unlike the military-options basket, acquires tradable value only as the negotiations proceed. This inevitably means that the protagonists of the CWC within the intragovernmental negotiations must defend a position that is bound to be weak (because it is uncertain) until the Geneva talks have advanced far enough for the options they propose to appear genuinely viable. Here we may see a more fundamental reason why the Geneva talks have taken so long in coming anywhere near fruition; and the fact that they have not come to collapse is testimony to the tenacity of the protagonists.

The explanation is this. The military self-reliance basket necessarily contains tangibles--stockpiles of chemical weapons, factories for making them, and so on--that have a self-evident worth to possessor governments: military options conferred, capital investment, employment, and more. In the international-collaboration basket there are no such tangibles, only the promise of their absence. The CWC protagonists are advocating the trade of something concrete for something abstract. They are proposing that the means for menacing adversaries with chemical weapons (or the retention of an open option for acquiring such weapons later on, should changing events make it seem prudent to do so) should be exchanged for the promise of not being so menaced by adversaries. Unless governments are prepared to place faith in one another's good intentions and in the permanence of those intentions, the international-collaboration basket must lack value until the negotiating partners--all of them, for they are all to collaborate in the regime--can begin to form an idea of the degree of assurance they will get that the promises will be fulfilled. Moreover, the military-industrial base from which a national capability to use chemical weapons could be derived is so diffuse and, in parts, so much an element of other military or industrial capabilities, that a high degree of assurance, which is to say a credible value for options in the international-collaboration basket, may require major concessions from all the negotiating partners. We can thus see why the matter of estblishing confidence in compliance with the regime lies at the very heart of the negotiations. A concept for addressing it must accordingly provide the core of our analytical framework.

Chapter 3. National security and the relative value of policy alternatives

How confidence in the projected Chemical Weapons Convention may best be built and sustained is the subject of chapter 5. Before entering that difficult terrain, we need to consider the question of value. What, we must ask, may be the yardstick against which the worth of international collaboration in the anti-CW regime can be measured and compared with the worth of the competing option of national self-reliance? What is the device that we may build into our analytical framework so that a particular basket of treaty proposals can be assessed for its merits against those of a particular basket of military options? At what points along the ranges of possible content for the two baskets may exchange of the one for the other be judged worthwhile? There is no simple answer.

Categories of value

Table 2 below provides a first cut into this complex matter. It illustrates some of the loci of the competing costs and benefits to a state. The table is not meant to be an exhaustive listing. It is intended only to display examples.

We can see at once from table 2 that there are several categories of value that may need to be taken into account: military, economic, social and political. We can also see that the level of analysis at which one category of value is adequately assessable is not necessarily the same as for another category. Thus, in some instances the costs and benefits are discernible at the macro level of the state itself. In other instances, they have significance only to certain social groupings at subordinate levels: to people and activities within particular sectors of the economy, say, or

Table 2. Significant elements of value associated with alternative options for national CW policy

National self-reliance

(1) Stocks of CW agents and devices for using them as weapons
(2) Military options conferred by (1), including the potential for deterring adversary resort to CW by threat of retaliation in kind
(3) Employment, career and commercial opportunities inherent in the activities required to supply (1), which is to say the activities exemplified in column (a) of table 1
(4) Career opportunities inherent in the activities required to sustain designated user-services in a state of readiness to exploit (1), which is to say the activities exemplified in column (b) of table 1
(5) Stocks of anti-chemical defence equipment for protection against the effects of chemical weapons, one´s own or an enemy´s
(6) Employment, career and commercial opportunities inherent in the activities required to supply or sustain readiness to use (5)
(7) Active monitoring of a scientific and technical domain from which security-significant technological surprise might emerge
(8) Tangible contributions facilitated for the support of military allies, as from (1), (5) and (7)

Collaboration in an international CW disarmament regime

(9) Denial of military options to potential enemies
(10) Preclusion of proliferation of chemical weapons
(11) Reduction of the fraction of the national wealth that must be spent on CW preparedness
(12) Heightened prospects for security-enhancing agreement in other areas of arms control and disarmament
(13) Elements from any adoption there may be of measures of national self-reliance that are not incompatible with the regime--that is, from (6)
(14) The stabilizing influence on international relations resulting from increased interdependence, extension of international law and diminished mass destruction potential

to particular departments of government. At these latter--micro--levels, we can see that a particular option may benefit one grouping and penalize another, in which case interests become vested in both the furtherance and the rejection of that option. Thus are created the interest groups and factions to which we have been referring. They will vary in the degree of influence they can command in the supreme councils of state, this providing the mechanism controlling the entry of factional costs and benefits into the overall assessment of value for the state as a whole. In states where the military, for example, is dominant politically, the military value of competing options is likely to count for more than in less militarized states. Again, we can see from table 2, as at (3), (4) or (6), that what is beneficial in economic or social terms at a some micro level--the level of an individual corporation, perhaps, or a geographical region or a profession--may display itself as a substantial cost--an opportunity cost--at the macro level.

The concept of national security

There is nothing about the problem of reconciling different scales and levels of value that is peculiar to CW policy options. With the growth of arms-control endeavour over the past 25 years in nuclear and non-nuclear fields alike, a conceptual device for coping with the problem has come into widespread currency: that of 'national security'. This is seemingly a concept of sufficient generality to subsume military, economic and social considerations while, at the same time, asserting a ranking principle whereby factional interests may be subordinated to a national imperative. If we were to use it in the present analysis (as we shall), we would do so in the following fashion: should a state judge that its national security would be served equally well either by commitment to a Chemical Weapons Convention having such-and-such a set of provisions or by measures of national self-reliance comprising the retention, with or without implementation, of such-and-such a set of military and related options, then that judgement would imply that the contents of the international-collaboration and national self-reliance baskets were, in the assessment of that state, at a breakeven point. Nothing of national importance would be lost by joining the Convention if those military options were the only ones that had currently been implemented.

As abstract concepts go, 'national security' has a notably persuasive appeal. Perhaps because of the power of the different sentiments that are embedded within it, people are prepared to defer to it almost as though it were something concrete, not abstract. Governments in even the most liberal of countries are able to cite it to justify actions of extraordinary illiberality. It is exactly that seemingly tangible and self-evident quality which suggests the concept as the yardstick for which we are seeking.

Yet, as a means for assessing value it can advance our analysis only if its limitations are recognized. One such limitation is that the concept has useful meaning only when it is taken in a relative sense--that is, in the sense of the national security being better served by this or that proceeding, a condition of the state that is liable to become enhanced or degraded in particular eventualities. In absolute terms the concept conveys little that has the precision or general acceptability that we need.

It might be supposed, for example, that the national security was the condition of affairs whose preservation served as the reason for the existence of national armed forces. But an absolute definition in those terms would carry the implication that the armed forces were not only the guardians of the national security but also its arbiters as well. It would thus ignore economic, cultural and other nonmilitary dimensions. Security is patently more than a matter of military might.

Determinants of national security

The more closely the concept is considered, the more apparent does it become that, at the national level, as at the individual level, what constitutes security is purely a matter of perception, the form in which it is perceived being determined by the situations and interests of the perceivers--which is no doubt why, in many writings, the terms 'national security' and 'national interest' are used interchangeably. In applying the concept, we must therefore not lose sight of the fact that different groups whose opinions are influential within a country cannot always be expected to have one and the same view as to what may or may not be important for the national security. Which particular view becomes dominant to the point of directing national security policy is a function of the nature of the body politic in the country in question. In other words, a judgement by a government about the worth to the national security of this or that basket of CWC provisions is at root a political decision, albeit one in which military, economic and social considerations will have been duly weighed.

It might seem to follow from this conclusion that application in a relative, not an absolute, sense may destroy the normative value to our analysis of the concept of national security, for the conflation of different scales of value that the concept would otherwise seem to offer now appears to be illusory: the judgement will still turn on the relative political influence of precisely the same interest groups, whether it be debated in the language of national security or any other. A mirror would therefore appear to be all that the concept offers for our analysis, not a yardstick.

Nor is that the only problem. In the Geneva negotiations themselves, delegations are making increasing resort to the concept (without attempting to define it) in stating their positions on particular issues. This we can see in the reference to, for example, 'balanced security' in relation to mutual destructions of stockpiles. We can see it also in the debate over the rights of states parties to bar entry into their territories of fact-finding missions. In fact, to judge from some of the draft treaty language that has been put forward, there is some danger that the concept, despite its utterly nonobjective character, may even find its way into the operative parts of the treaty-text itself.

Be that as it may, the concept can still assist our analysis. For there is a second relative sense in which it may be used: security in relation to a threat. By applying the concept in recognition that intrinsic to it is the concept of threat, we may indeed find that common ground whereon the disparate and often competing claims of affected groups are resolvable through logical argument, thus affording a rationale for the requisite subordination of group interests to the overall national interest. A particular group may well claim that the opinion to which it holds, or the mission which it serves, is essential for the national security. But unless that group can also demonstrate the nature and the magnitude of the threat to the national security should its opinion be rejected or its mission be curtailed, its claims can carry little force against others where the threat is both demonstrable and significant.

The central role of threat analysis

A yardstick for assessing value thus begins to take shape. It seems a good one, not because it is to be supposed that governmental decision-making necessarily proceeds by rational argument, nor yet because threat-analysis--although it is now a rather well developed intellectual discipline--necessarily possesses sufficient rigour to display any one threat-evaluation as obviously either correct or incorrect; but rather because it brings consideration of the military utility of chemical weapons into the centre of our analysis, which is where it surely belongs. Between that utility and the requisites for the provisions of a worthwhile Chemical Weapons Convention there has to be a relationship of some directness and importance. The security yardstick shows us the form of that relationship, for it is the military utility of chemical weapons that, at root, defines the threat which CW may pose to the national security, and therefore also the relative value of alternative ways of mitigating that threat, whether they be measures of national self-reliance or international collaboration or both.

What we are saying here, then, is that our choice of national security as the measuring instrument for assessing value requires that we calibrate the instrument against the magnitude of the threats which the available options may serve to counter. So, to take our analysis a stage further, we must now consider more closely the nature of those threats.

From table 2 it is apparent that there are two broad categories of threat which we must address: threats that are and threat that are not directly associated with the continuing existence of chemical weapons. That the second category should require our attention at all may at first seem surprising. It is, however, a perfectly logical consequence of our use of the national-security concept, for CW policies of national self-reliance and of international collaboration can both serve the national security in ways that go beyond mitigating the CW threat by countering other threats too. Take, for example, the various costs and benefits to different social groups associated with elements (8), (12) and (14) in table 2. Some or all of them may well be highly significant to the groups concerned and, therefore, depending upon the political influence of those groups, require due consideration in the overall governmental assessment. It follows that, if the assessment is to be rationalized in security terms, the criterion of security must not be drawn so tightly as to exclude them. The threats to the national security to which those three elements may be seen as relating are not direct CW threats. They are, instead, diminished alliance cohesion (element 8), the adverse consequences of an uncontrolled arms race (element 12), and a poorly predictable, anarchical and generally hostile environment within which to conduct international relations (element 14).

The existence of this second, and wider, category of threat serves to remind us again of the looseness of the concept of national security. For it indicates that nations may be able to enhance their security, not only by building up armed forces to match the perceived military threats emanating from others, but also by co-operating in networks of economic, cultural and other intercourse whereby each gradually becomes dependent on the others, ultimately to the point where a threat to one becomes a threat to all. Herein lies, of course, that differentiation between 'defensive' or 'antagonistic' security on the one hand and, on the other, 'co-operative' or 'common' security [13, 14]: a differentiation which seems to offer a way out from that logic of nuclear deterrence on which the rich countries of the world--East and West alike--have been driven by domestic interests to rest their security.

Measured against a yardstick of national security which admits notions of common security as well as defensive security, an international-collaboration basket of CW policy options is bound to appear more valuable than if such notions were excluded. Yet just as arms control and common security lie so close to one another that the pursuit of the one is tantamount to pursuit of the other, so also may a bad arms-control agreement vitiate notions of common security. A CWC that was incapable of maintaining confidence in the international regime it had created--incapable of sustaining confidence in compliance--could destroy not only the pre-existing anti-CW regime but also much of the contiguous structure of common security. Shortcomings in the regime could very rapidly force states back into CW policies of national self-reliance, strengthening, in the process, the domestic power of interests affronted by all forms of arms control.

It follows, therefore, that our analysis can best exploit the concept of national security as a measure of value only if the concept is applied in its restrictive sense: in the sense of security against the threats that emanate from the continuing existence of chemical weapons. The nature of these threats must accordingly be the next subject of our inquiry.

Chapter 4. The threats posed by chemical weapons

We suggested in chapter 1 that the relative rarity of chemical warfare might be taken less as evidence that the anti-CW regime has been strong and more as evidence that chemical weapons have rarely been judged useful by the military. If frequency of use were an expression of preference, it would be clear that, for their weapons, the military prefer to exploit the physical destruction available from sources of kinetic and thermal energy, not the solely life-threatening or 'biospecific' [15] damage available from toxicity. Bullets, blast, fragmentation and flame are casualty agents which are more manageable than poison. They can be employed against targets more varied than animate ones alone. The relative ease of antichemical protection makes poison still less useful. We may also note the deep-rooted psychological aversions to poison which presumably contribute to the widespread sentiment that use of poison is contrary to the ethos of the military profession: underhand, ignoble and unchivalrous. We may thus understand why CW lies outside the mainstream of military theory and practice, its isolation at the periphery being conserved by that singular array of moral and legal proscriptions which constitutes the present international anti-CW regime.

Yet within a broad historical perspective, that outcaste status can appear merely as the hesitation which the military have traditionally displayed before accepting radically new types of weaponry. Flame weapons, gunpowder, even the crossbow, experienced lengthy periods of military disfavour and moral opprobrium before becoming assimilated into military doctrine and forces. The technical complexity of CW and, especially, the protective measures that are available against it may explain why those traditional inhibitions have taken so long to fall away from chemical weapons. Whether this is or is not sufficient explanation, it is clear that the present-day CW threat is heavily conditioned by its past. It therefore makes sense to define it by going back to the origins of present-day CW in World War I and then following events forward. It is convenient to structure such an historical survey according to the military, the technical and then the institutional origins of today's CW threat.

Military origins

The record of use of poisons in special-purpose weapons goes back some three millenia. But the technology which allowed their employment in conjunction with conventional battlefield weapons did not begin to appear until about a century ago.

The growth of chemical technology during the latter part of the nineteenth century had carried clear practical implications for the nature of future warfare, most conspicuous in the rapidity of innovation in the field of explosives and propellants. That toxic chemicals might come to contribute to weaponry more extensively than in the past was appreciated earlier--or so it seems--outside the military profession than within it, so much so that at intergovernmental conferences in Brussels (1874) and The Hague (1899 and 1907) specific measures of CW arms control were included among the agreements reached. Military and naval establishments began to consider the possibilities seriously during the rearmament period preceding World War I. By the end of 1914, primitive chemical weapons for infantry and artillery forces had been introduced onto the European battlefield by both France and Germany [16], and others were under development in Britain [17]. All of these early weapons were, however, carefully designed so as not to contravene the letter of the existing prohibitions. The impact of the weapons was evidently extremely slight, for scarcely any reference to them exists even in the most detailed histories of the war.

The initial resort to CW on a large scale was by Germany in April 1915, in a form which had apparently not been envisaged by the draftsmen of the Hague prohibitions. Germany had, at that time, a virtual monopoly in the facilitating technology, that of the large-scale liquefaction of chlorine gas, for which there was much demand in the rapidly ascendant German chemical industry. By exploiting the area-effectiveness and permeating characteristics of the airborne clouds of poison that could be discharged from cylinders of liquid chlorine, the protagonists of this new method of warfare hoped to relieve two constraints under which German forces were operating. The new weapon could, it was believed, provide a means both for reducing demand for explosives (the supply of raw materials for which was threatened by the British naval blockade) and for restoring that mobility to the battlefield which had been destroyed by trench-warfare tactics. The latter had been adopted to counter the massive firepower of machine-guns and artillery exploiting the new propellants and high explosives.

The 'off-target' or 'cloud gas' CW technique of releasing airborne poison upwind of the target area did indeed prove, at the Second Battle of Ypres, to have a mass-casualty effect. It encouraged further attention to those early 'on-target' techniques of the previous year, in which toxic-fill artillery or mortar projectiles were fired directly into the target area, thus providing a less weather-dependent form of attack. However, countermeasures that provided protection against CW attack were speedily developed, principally individual-issue respirators (gas masks) to filter poison out of inhaled air. Until mid-1917 significant tactical success with chemical weapons was attainable only by creating crash concentrations of CW agent from massed on-target delivery systems. The British developed a notably effective weapon for this purpose in the 'Livens Projector', which was an improvised large-calibre mortar used in batteries of several dozen, the operational counterpart of which today is the multiple-launch rocket system. As it happened, the general lack of confidence in CW fire-support then prevailing among British field commanders meant that the Livens Projector was rarely used for anything more than attrition.

In July 1917, at the Third Battle of Ypres, Germany introduced mustard gas, a still more effective counter-countermeasure that caused delayed mass casualties through its attack either as vapour or as liquid droplets on exposed skin and eyes. By the end of the war, the competition between chemical weapons and antichemical protection significantly favoured the former, though in general only in defensive operations, and military commanders had acquired greater confidence in chemical weapons, which were then being used on a swiftly increasing scale. Poison gas was moving towards assimilation as a conventional weapon.

But World War I also called forth the tank and the ground-attack aircraft, and during the next two decades these brought about as profound a realignment of the firepower-mobility-dispersion triad that dictates battlefield doctrine as had machine-guns and high explosives earlier. The latter had created a battlefield favouring CW, but the new tactical doctrines could accommodate the chemical weapons of the period only with difficulty, and therefore at substantial opportunity cost to other forms of military capability. This was because the available CW agents (dominated by phosgene, which was the successor to chlorine, and mustard gas) were too slow-acting and logistically too demanding to be easily suited to mobile ground warfare. Only against primitive opposition was poison gas seen to have definite value; and it has been in this context, and this context alone, that chemical weapons have been used since World War I, as, during the interwar years, in Russia (1919), Morocco (1925), Sinkiang (1934), Ethiopia (1935-39) and China (1937-42).

Other than that 'downhill' [18] utility, military interest in CW languished after World War I, this being displayed in an unwillingness to commit substantial resources to its further development or to exploit such developments as did come about, most notably in Germany and Britain. These attitudes also coloured appreciations of poison gas as the strategic weapon then being anticipated by fiction-writers and publicists for various causes. It is true that capabilities for counter-city CW attacks were built up to relatively advanced degrees of operational readiness. This reflected, we may perhaps suppose, the lesser opportunity costs of CW capability to air forces as compared with ground forces. But in actual operational planning for aerial bombardment, the inclinations of the planners, especially after the Spanish Civil War, were towards mass use of high-explosive and incendiary bombs, not poison gas. There seems to have been no concerted opposition from military staffs towards the CW prohibitions of the international anti-CW regime, now newly extended via the 1925 Geneva Protocol and reflected in national CW policies. During World War II, the existence of retaliatory capabilities was announced from time to time as a deterrent; but in fact there was never any great military incentive for such deterrents to constrain, and the stocks of poison gas for air and ground weapons alike remained essentially unused. By the end of the war, chemical weapons were viewed more as an awkward remnant of history than as a useful implement of tactical or strategic warfare, now likely to be dominated by nuclear weapons.

Post-war technical developments, primarily the further development of tabun and the other extraordinarily deadly 'nerve gases' which the victors had discovered in the laboratories and arsenals of defeated Germany, caused some reappraisal of the military value of CW. Nerve-gas weapons, especially those that might be based on sarin, soman and the still newer V agents, were clearly less unsuited than their predecessors to mobile warfare, being faster acting and effective in smaller quantities. Yet, at least in the West, the military leaders of the time remained predisposed against CW and, rightly or wrongly, continued to judge the weapons as more of a nuisance than an asset. Such advocacy of chemical weaponry as there was in Western military circles was influential only to the extent of bringing about minor concessions, so far as can be seen only transient ones. In the USA, for example, the national CW policy of no-first-use was secretly shifted by the Eisenhower Administration to one of use-at-the-President's-discretion, but was shifted back again in 1969 by President Nixon.

Whether the situation has been any different in the USSR, we have no certain means of telling. Since 1938, Soviet leaders have made no direct reference in public to their CW employment policy, and have maintained stringent control over information about their CW programmes and deployments. The state of ignorance that has thus been created outside the Soviet leadership has exacerbated the ever-present tendency in the West to believe the worst of the USSR. This, coupled with inferences drawn from what can be seen of Soviet antichemical protective measures and from such secret intelligence as is available, has led many authoritative commentators to perceive a high degree of Soviet readiness to exploit CW wherever and whenever that might be favoured by military circumstances. The Soviet CW stance is perceived, in short, as unconstrained by the present international anti-CW regime, notwithstanding repeated Soviet declarations of support for that regime. This view of the Soviet CW situation, which is to be found outside the Western alliance as well as within it, has been described in numerous Soviet publications as false and slanderous. But Moscow seems to have made no attempt to redress the state of ignorance about actual Soviet CW capabilities which fosters so mistrustful a view.

Technical origins

From a technical standpoint, we may see the chemical weapons of today as the product of four broad influences: changing target characteristics, evolving antichemical protection, the availability of new poisons, and changing weapon delivery systems. Of these it is surely the second that is far and away the most important technical determinant of the CW threat.

Were CW to be fought today between the forces now deployed in Europe, the situation would be very different from that in 1918, for the ascendancy of the offence over the defence--the weapons over the protective countermeasures--is now largely reversed. Noncombatant CW casualties would be vastly more numerous because the greater toxicity of modern CW agents (the nerve gases) would mean that clouds of poison would drift much longer distances downwind of their targets before becoming diluted to harmlessness; and civilians are no more likely to be issued with effective antichemical protection today than they were then. But the quality of modern military respirators, the development and general issue of protective clothing capable of keeping out mustard gas and skin-penetrative nerve gases, and the antichemical protective doctrines now taught by the military all suggest that the casualty-rates among combatants would now be much lower for the expenditure of a given weight of chemical munitions than they would be for the same weight of conventional munitions. Chemical weapons would thus no longer have much value as an element of firepower that could be relied upon for the attrition of enemy forces. Their tactical value would reside, not in their direct effects on enemy forces, but in the less predictable impact which the protective measures they would call forth might have on enemy combat efficiency. That impact would reside (a) in the cumbrousness of respirators and protective clothing, notably the obstacles created by gloves and masks to the use of weapons and instruments; (b) in the thermal load and attendant risk of heat stress in hot weather; (c) in the time delays imposed by the necessity of detoxifying or abandoning work-areas and equipments contaminated with persistent CW agents capable of attacking through the skin; and (d) in reductions of group cohesion and morale. In some circumstances such degradation might prove of great tactical significance, amounting, in effect, to an indirect attrition of enemy forces, a reduction of their ability to manoeuvre and a major constraint on the tempo with which they could conduct offensive operations. In other circumstances the degradation might prove no more than a nuisance.

How frequently degradation might have the former type of impact in comparison with the latter is a matter for detailed scenario-based operational analysis. In its absence, and in the absence, more especially, of those empirical data from properly designed field-exercises without which such analysis is largely futile, the magnitude of this form of CW threat cannot properly be assessed. Given the strongly subjective character of the assumptions that would have to go into such assessments, it may be expected that opinions will differ widely. It would be an imprudent person indeed who accepted uncritically any one particular opinion.

Two things may be asserted with some confidence, however. One is that there is a law of rapidly diminishing returns governing the relationship between the weight of chemical munitions expended in order to impose degradation and the tactical benefit thereby derived. A large supply of chemical weapons in the hands of an enemy may thus be no more threatening than a rather small supply. It is high time, we may observe here, that quantitative studies of this matter became available in the open literature. The other is that the degree of degradation, and hence either the value of imposing it or the magnitude of the threat that it represents, is bound to diminish--though not to a vanishing point--as technical development continues to reduce the burden of antichemical protection. This, too, is surely a matter which the CW arms-control community should long ago have investigated closely.

Might not such a trend in protection, however, be upset, as in the past, by some new development on the offensive side of CW technology? The key point to observe is that the efficacy of current antichemical protection stems from its exploitation of physical, not chemical, principles in the first line of defence. With the exception of small-molecule agents, against which special chemical impregnants can be incorporated, the efficacy of the filter in a gas mask or the air inlet of a shelter is essentially independent of the chemical nature of the challenge. Whatever the identity of the CW agent, known or unknown, filters can be relied upon to retain all but perhaps a millionth part of it, whether it be in vapour or aerosol form. Even for some hypothetical future CW agent active at a thousandth of the dosage of a nerve gas, the fraction penetrating would be far too small to be significant. Only if the agent--or an adjuvant disseminated with it--were capable of subverting the physical mechanisms of filtration might the threat alter significantly. Although the possibilities here are not negligible, they are limited, and are therefore, like the related possibilities for overwhelming protective clothing, relatively easy to monitor.

We may suppose that it is primarily because antichemical protection can negate so much of the direct effectiveness of chemical weapons that CW has found most of its application against primitive opposition lacking the requisite technology. Wars characterized by such asymmetry do not appear to be diminishing in frequency, and will no doubt continue to generate incentive for resort to CW. Their nature has in the past created requirements for special types of toxic weapon, and this too may continue to influence the technical character of the CW threat. Counterinsurgency tactics, for example, have greatly increased the prominence of the category of incapacitating chemical weapons--weapons based on toxic agents capable of disabling people without themselves imposing high mortality rates or the necessity of medical treatment on noncombatants intermingled with them, rather as police forces use tear gas to avoid the domestic political costs of resort to deadly weapons. A related category of technical innovation comprises chemical weapons in which the poisons used are maximally toxic against plant life, not against people. Used in guerrilla warfare, such herbicidal weapons may be, and have been, targeted on food crops thought to sustain guerrilla forces in the field or against the vegetation that provides them with concealment. Certain other target characteristics that might engender further forms of toxic weaponry can be envisaged. For example, where war aims might be furthered by terrorization, demoralization or coercion of civilian populations, toxic agents capable of eliciting conspicuous, powerful and lasting but not inevitably lethal damage over a broad range of field dosages might seem to offer a form of force more efficient in the absence of antichemical protection than any other.

The magnitude of the threat which these categories of, respectively, incapacitant, herbicidal and terrorizing chemical weapons represent to a state is not easy to assess in terms of the national security. In fact, there are evidently some national authorities that see some of these weapons as more of an asset than a threat, presumably because the weapons could prove valuable to internal-security forces. Hence the endeavours, which still continue, to suggest that in a sense which is significant for the purposes of the Chemical Weapons Convention they are not in fact chemical weapons. However, because their target effects all reside in their toxicity, their differentiation from other more traditional categories of chemical weapon appears to be impossible on technical grounds alone. This is discussed further in chapter 6.

Institutional origins

In the history of national CW programmes since World War I, there is, within a particular set of countries, a feature of such apparent consistency from country to country and of such peculiar oddity that we must give it special attention. It is the contrast between, on the one hand, a lack of serious military interest in CW and, on the other hand, a continual allocation of resources into chemical-weapons programmes. There is a disjunction here whose explanation must surely bear on the nature of today's CW threat. That explanation seems to lie in the institutional underpinning of national CW programmes.

It is apparent to any student of technology acquisition in the field of national armament that the process whereby new weapons enter the arsenals has a push-pull dynamic: burgeoning technology at one end and changing military requirements at the other. An objective of good defence management is to keep the two in balance. One interpretation of the disjunction just noted is that CW armament is a case where the push of technology preponderates over the pull of military requirements. More research needs to be done on this conception of supply outrunning demand, but what is at least *prima facie* evidence in support of it may be found in state papers dealing with CW armament in US, British and German national archives.

Further, such documentation suggests that an explanation for the strength of the technological impulse is to be found in the operation of institutional factors. During World War I, the waging of CW required each belligerent to create a supporting infrastructure of R&D establishments, headquarters directorates, CW-specialty service commands, production capacity, and the like. New institutions thus came into existence; and because they were highly specialized, the livelihood, ambitions and career patterns of their occupants inevitably became intertwined to some degree with their special mission. They thus acquired a self-propagating character. During the post-war contraction of military effort, governments found it easier to run down the institutions than to close them out altogether, the latter option in any case being unattractive for other reasons. Thus established (with different degrees of autonomy and coherence in different countries), the CW institutions were able to find sustenance within the prevailing currents of legislative and administrative or bureaucratic politics, capitalizing on favourable ebbs and flows in technology (such as the emergence of new weapons-delivery systems) or military requirements (such as colonial policing). When military requirements for chemical weapons declined, there was still a continuing requirement for some form of antichemical protective posture, necessitating continuing attention to offensive CW. During the pre-World War II rearmament period, it was thus virtually inevitable that part of the across-the-board increases in military appropriations should come to revitalize moribund chemical-weapons programmes: though the military logic might be weak, the institutional logic was strong. The growth of CW armament at that time may thus be seen at least in part as an inevitable consequence of the way large organizations behave.

Nor was it difficult for the CW institutions to provide a justifying rationale for this growth. Did not the existence of the new Geneva Protocol positively require the maintenance of a CW retaliatory capability in order to deter violation so that the rule of international law might be upheld? This was a powerful argument, not so much because of its assertion that CW could deter CW, nor even because international law necessarily demanded respect, but rather because it responded to a feeling widely sensed in different quarters: a feeling that, even though <u>we</u> might see no great reason for having chemical weapons ourselves, our enemies, being more devious people, might have done so, so perhaps we should keep some as a safeguard: a safeguard, not so much against enemy CW, though that could be sensible too, but against our military advisers being wrong, or against some eventuality as yet unforeseen.

Such feelings became strongly damped during the years after World War II by the rapid shrinking of military expenditures and by the confirmation which that war seemed to have provided that chemical weapons were an irrelevant leftover of World War I. Chemical disarmament was, accordingly, not limited to the vanquished powers alone.

But there were other countries where the CW institutions were able to impress upon their masters the view that the technological advances which had been made in the CW field during the war had not yet been developed to the point where such dismissive evaluations of CW were necessarily tenable. During the period 1936-41 there had been, we may now see, three really major technical advances, all of them coming too late, given the circumstances, for practical application during World War II. One of them was the discovery, in an industrial laboratory concerned with pesticides, of the first member of the family of poisons now called 'nerve gases'. Another was the demonstration in military field experiments that cultures of pathogenic micro-organisms could, like poisons, be disseminated in a casualty-threatening airborne form from munitions adaptable to conventional weapon systems. The third was the discovery, again in an industrial laboratory, that certain of the synthetic chemicals by then being studied in several parts of the world as mimics of natural plant-growth hormone were also capable of disrupting plant growth, and of doing so to such an extent and in such a manner that the chemicals might be used to reduce drastically the yields of many staple food crops at application densities well within the capacity of contemporary military aircraft--at densities rather smaller, it later transpired, than those that would probably be needed to kill people with nerve gas. Had these discoveries occurred earlier, at a time when military interest in chemical weapons would still have been great enough to command the resources and priorities required for their speedy full-scale development, and then for their integration into force-structure and doctrine, the status of CW during World War II might well have been very different.

So it was that, after the war, it was argued that all of these developments portended important new military utilities for commodities that the CW institutions, if kept running, might be able to provide: utilities which, far from being outmoded by nuclear warfare, could complement it. Even though--so the available archives indicate--military authorities remained generally sceptical and unenthusiastic, these claims of untapped potential were accepted to the point of allowing the CW institutions a new lease of life. A new momentum began to build up in their programmes, impelled by the deepening mistrusts of the Cold War and the widespread feeling, born out of World War II, that all scientific inquiry should be fostered in the cause of the national security. With military budgets once again fattening, the chemical (and biological) armament programmes of those countries soon moved into fullscale production.

Those programmes of chemical-warfare rearmament began in secret, and their subsequent course, even whether they still continue, has remained that way except for the US programme. One consequence of the opening for broader scrutiny, in the latter 1960s, of the US rearmament was that its protagonists were, for the first time in decades, required to justify the programme in current security terms. The argument was again that of in-kind CW deterrence. In view of the CW no-first-use regime, that is of course the only justification that can be produced in public--whether by the USA or by her consorts in the post-1950 CW rearmament, France and the USSR. Whether for the two latter countries the argument would be <u>ex post</u> rationalization for programmes driven by the institutional pressure of supply, or whether it would be an accurate portrayal of motives underlying genuinely demand-led programmes, it is of course impossible for us to tell.

In one sense it is also irrelevant, for it is the fact that the offensive CW capabilities exist, not how they came to exist, that is important to our threat analysis. But in other senses, it is highly relevant. It may tell us, first, whether institutional pressure might be strong enough to vitiate hopes for the creation of a viable CW disarmament regime. Second, it may tell us more about whether the primary option that would be foreclosed by such a regime--that of in-kind CW deterrence--is or is not a valuable one.

Yet that last question, like so many similar ones having to do wih the efficacy of deterrence, can only be answered--short of the test of war itself--by an act of faith; and there will as usual be firm believers, weak believers, sceptics and agnostics. Some may point to the abstention from CW during World War II as a confirmation of their belief, yet close examination of the available historical record shows that that is but poor evidence. On the various occasions when contingency (and other) plans for the initiation of CW were formulated and filtered through the command channels of the Western Allies, they were more often than not rejected for reasons having nothing to do with Axis CW capabilities. There were, it is true, other instances when Axis CW capabilities were cited as reason for scrapping the plans, but in all such instances the deterrent threat perceived was that of counter-city CW attack, even in response to tactical use on the battlefield. Between nuclear-weapon states or nuclear alliances, such threats are no longer credible. There seems to be no evidence at all that may be drawn from World War II that in-kind CW deterrence works at less escalatory levels of threatened retaliation. Maybe it really would work on the battlefield; but that is as yet neither proven nor disproven. Poison gas was not used during World War II because of the rarity of the occasions on which it could, on purely military grounds, be the preferred weapon. And when those rare occasions did arise, the degree of military preparedness actually to exploit poison gas in the manner required was simply insufficient [19]. Deterrence at the strategic level perhaps contributed to that lack of preparedness, but only as one factor among several.

Synthesis

We may see the nature of today's CW threat to the security of states in terms of two main components: the concrete here-and-now component arising from the fact that, for many countries, powerful chemical weapons actually exist in the arsenals of potential adversaries; and the more abstract future component arising from the fact that both CW technology and military perceptions of need for it are in a state of flux.

Intelligence and the current threat

The precise nature of the first component is definable by a state within the limitations of its CW-intelligence capacity. The threat is determined by the size, the lethality and the deployment of the stocks of poison gas, and by the nature of the delivery systems with which the poisons could be used. However, the greater the limitations on the intelligence of such matters, the greater (not the less) is the threat likely to appear. There are three types of limitation. First, the available data are bound to be insufficient, either because of the extent to which those data are held secure, or because of an insufficiency of assets dedicated to their collection. Second, there will be analytical limitations. Interpretation and evaluation of fragmentary data need special skills and experience which may not be available; and a degree of comprehension of CW technicalities is required that may be available only from CW institutions, in which case there may be the further complication of the evaluation becoming coloured by institutional interests. Third, there will be methodological limitations. The available data will relate mainly to adversary capabilities, yet it is in adversary intentions that the reality of the threat resides. While the latter may be inferable from the former, that will be an uncertain process at best, for capabilities may, as we have seen, be more a reflection of institutional pressure than of military requirement, coupled though the two may be. So even assuming that the available CW-intelligence capacity is capable of delineating the magnitude of adversary CW capability, it may still be unable to determine the degree of threat which inevitably resides in, for example, the possibility of retaliatory capability being used to initiate CW. This we shall return to later in this chapter. For future reference (in chapters 5 and 6), we may flag here the notion of the CWC regime being designed in such a way as to enhance CW-intelligence capacity, thereby reducing the dangers to the regime that could flow from erroneous assessments of threat.

Assimilation and the future threat

As for the character of the future CW threat, we can do no more than point to trends. Two broad types may be discerned. First, outside trends in the environment inhabited by the CW institutions: developments in that wider domain of military theory and practice, of industrial enterprise, of scientific inquiry, and of political attitudes which may by chance stimulate innovation in CW armament. Several of these we have alluded to already, for example the possibility of structural change in the chemical and allied manufacturing industries altering the balance of relative accessibility--that is, cost--of toxic biotechnological-process products, say, as compared with today's CW agents, which rely heavily on petrochemicals. We may also note here, as another example of such exogenous trends, one of the consequences of security having been rested more and more heavily, since the advent of nuclear weapons, on deterrence. In the days when the military existed primarily for the purpose of fighting wars, their professional codes of behaviour on what was and was not an acceptable method of fighting had a real impact on the conduct of war. The fact that poison gas was regarded as an ignoble and unchivalrous weapon meant that it was less likely to be used. Deterrence doctrine has lowered the expectation within the military profession that it will actually be called upon to fight. Deterrence has, at the same time, put a premium on increasing the horrors of war should it nonetheless happen. Infamous weapons may thereby be gaining in acceptability [20].

The second broad type are those trends which are inherent in the existing dynamic of CW technology, ones with which the CW institutions are already intimately familiar. There are two primary examples. The first example is the trend that the CW institutions have been nurturing since their earliest days, that of producing weapons whose effects or operating requirements may serve to lessen their opportunity costs to conventional forces. The new US 'binary' nerve-gas munitions (see pages 82-83 below) are the latest embodiment of this particular trend, their possibility of diminished opportunity cost residing in their lesser storage and handling hazards claimed for them by their proponents, which, also, could increase the likelihood of their being accepted into the basic tactical load of fighting units. The second example is the equally long-standing competition between offence and defence: of finding new ways of breaching antichemical protection. This is the trend that should, for the moment, be taken the most seriously of all, not because the possibility of some major new counter-countermeasure emerging appears particularly imminent, but because, if it were to emerge, it might alter the whole calculus of the military value of CW. This, too, is a matter of great importance to the CWC regime which we should also flag here for future reference.

We should not belittle the importance of the future component of the CW threat; yet we may nonetheless observe that the technology of chemical armament has remained remarkably static for the past three decades. Apart from that continuing, if still remote, possibility of some sudden upheaval in the offence-defence balance, it seems that the real longer term danger is a more hidden one. It lies in the fact that the weapon-development motors are still running within institutional frameworks that could ultimately bring about a more favourable orientation of military attitudes towards CW, attitudes which may spread to countries that have so far shown no particular interest in chemical weapons. A fashion for CW could grow. This component of the threat may thus be seen more generally to derive from the future course of that process of assimilation which, when conceived as an historical process, has evidently not yet progressed to completion. In practical terms, the future threat might manifest itself either as an overt conventionalization of chemical weapons within the arsenals of the advanced industrialized countries, or as a proliferation of the weapons to other parts of the world. Let us therefore register here a third notion worth developing further: that of the CWC regime being conceived, among its primary objectives, as a constraint on the assimilation process.

Supply-side threats

What we are saying here is that it might make a lot of sense to assess the various components of today's CW threat in terms of a second categorization as well. Thus, the threat may be assessed in terms not only of the in-being/potential categories just discussed, but also in terms of threats which do or do not originate solely in the response of a potential adversary's institutions of supply to enunciated military requirements: a distinction between supply-determined and demand-determined threats. Such a distinction has little to offer when the question is one of the military options that are needed to counter the overall CW threat, for those options must be responsive to the actualities of the threat, not its origins. But it is highly relevant to the options afforded by the current negotiations for a CWC, because it illuminates the mechanisms of confidence in the projected treaty regime.

Above all, the distinction may be used to define ways in which individual states may, by their own actions, project assurance to other states that certain otherwise highly ambiguous activities are not in fact threatening. Such ambiguities are especially liable to generate mistrust when they suggest that a particular programme under surveillance could result in military capabilities that confer illicit military options. There are two very prominent examples in today's CW world. One is the prosecution by Country A of an equipment programme in the field of antichemical protection which seems to Country B to confer far more protection to A's force posture--a much greater capacity for fighting within a CW-contaminated environment--than would be needed to counter the chemical weapons of Country B or of any other of Country A's potential adversaries. The programme may then seem evidence of A's intention to use its own chemical weapons whenever that might be militarily expedient. The second example is that of Country A moving to counter what it sees as an increasing obsolescence of its CW retaliatory capability by producing new chemical munitions better suited than their predecessors to the latest conventional delivery systems or to newly evolved doctrines of conventional warfare; a programme which Country B might again interpret as A seeking to conventionalize CW. In both cases, that might indeed be the intention of Country A, in which case B would be justified in perceiving a new threat and responding accordingly. But it might also be that the institutions of supply in Country A were over-responding--inadvertently or intentionally--to military needs, overfulfilling military requirements, thereby creating an appearance of threat which was in fact false or which otherwise deceived the intelligence of Country B. Here, then, is a context in which national means of control--such as have long figured at least in principle in the Geneva negotiations--could have special value, provided such means could both have the effect and be seen to have the effect of limiting the institutional pressure of supply.

It is also a context in which we may discern a negative consequence of the Geneva negotiations. For if the negotiations are seen by participating governments as a means to some wider or different end than CW arms-control agreement, then their subject--chemical weapons--acquires a new value to the foreign policies of those governments. A new utility for chemical weapons has thus been called into being to augment those which, if we are correct in seeing chemical weapons as supply-led armament, are otherwise sparse. The supply of 'bargaining chips' may soon become transformed into a demand for them.

Such considerations have the effect, which must surely be a salutary one, of suggesting that progress towards an effective Chemical Weapons Convention may not depend solely on the behaviour of other states: that there may be a good deal of room for productive unilateral actions too, whether they are or are not reciprocated.

Ranking levels of threat

Supply-led armament is by definition unassimilated armament. The significance of the existing anti-CW regime is that its imposition upon states of at least a no-first-use policy obstructs full assimilation of CW armament. Maybe the regime will not count for much in the crisis of war; but, even so, national armed services can have less expectation of using the weapons than they do of other weapons not constrained by no-first-use policies. Their incentive to integrate chemical weapons fully into posture and doctrine--to allocate resources to preparations and training for use of the weapons--is correspondingly weakened. Yet if those armed services that possess the weapons have not integrated them fully, their display of preparedness and resolve for the retaliation-in-kind whereby they are avowedly discouraging adversaries from resorting to CW may be unconvincing, in which case they can have no real confidence in their expectation of non-use. The no-first-use regime has thus created a deep contradiction within national CW armament programmes, which, because it necessarily complicates the task of managing those programmes efficiently, must significantly affect the reality of the CW threat. The contradictions may be seen as generating pressure on national CW policy which could push the latter in one or other of two opposite directions: resolve the contradiction by abandoning the armament, or resolve it by abandoning the no-first-use policy. It can be expected that there will be partisans of both approaches within the military establishment of the country in question, in which case there should exist a significant degree of shared interest between the arms-control community, seeking to preserve and if possible extend the anti-CW regime, and a part of the military community.

The question for the future is whether such concord is sufficient to support a worthwhile Chemical Weapons Convention. We can see that it could vanish very quickly if demand-side factors grew in influence, for then the alternative route out of the contradiction could gain increased support. We may expect such growth to find its strongest stimulus in wars in the developing regions of the world, for there the constraint which antichemical protection imposes on the military utility of chemical weapons is likely to be at its weakest.

If that is so, it follows that chemical weapons that are adapted more to the combat requirements of such wars than to those of warfare in, say, Europe should be regarded by all states as a substantial part of the overall CW threat, at least in its future aspect. Even though such weapons may represent no direct danger to the security of an industrialized country, and may indeed be seen as a positive asset by those governments that think in terms of 'projecting power' into distant regions, they constitute a mechanism whereby more directly dangerous manifestations of CW threat may increase in immediacy. The 'yellow rain' affair has already provided a concrete illustration: we have seen from it how reports of mycotoxin warfare in southeast Asia, whether they be true or false, have made many people more conscious of the possibilities of nerve-gas warfare in Europe.

The incapacitating, herbicidal and other forms of chemical weaponry that are especially suited to North-South or Third World conflict may therefore constitute significant elements of CW threat to the security of all nations. To the North, their threat is an indirect, not a direct, one, so its degree may be ranked rather lower than that of nerve-gas and mustard-gas weaponry. To some regions of the South, in contrast, the threat-ranking might be at much the same level. Where does that leave the other categories of chemical weapon? On the foregoing reasoning, would not all those classes of chemical weapon that found application in World War I represent a comparable degree of menace? The answer is surely not, for most of them would fall foul of a basic military criterion no less applicable outside the domain of advanced industrialized warfare as it is within it. The decision to resort to chemical weapons is a decision which judges their usefulness in the situation concerned to be greater than that of other weapons, a matter which is reducible--though by no means completely so--to cost-effectiveness calculation. Even when antichemical protection is not deployed, few of the World War I CW agents seem likely to provide munitions today that would measure up at all well against the cost-effectiveness of the huge variety of conventional munitions, even the less sophisticated types, currently available from the world's arms manufacturers. In comparison with, for example, napalm, fragmentation warheads or the simpler forms of cluster munition, weapons disseminating the lung gases, the blood gases or the arsenicals (though not mustard gas) would surely fail this basic test of military value. This does not mean that these older classes of CW agent can be dismissed entirely as threats, for considerations of psychological impact or accessibility might perhaps still tilt the decision in their favour; but they are threats of what clearly appears to be a lesser order of magnitude.

Chapter 5. Assurance and Verification

Policy options against chemical threats

The threat of chemical weapons to the security of a state may, we can thus see, present a variety of aspects. An aspect that appears less dangerous or less immediate or less direct to one state may not appear so to another. So the type of CW policy that suits one state may not suit another. Defence, deterrence or both are the national measures of self-reliance against chemical weapons.

The route of defence seeks to neutralize the threat by countermeasures that deprive it of effectiveness. These countermeasures reside in the armed forces which the state maintains to counter any form of enemy attack, whether delivered by chemical or other means. The better the antichemical protective equipments with which the forces are supplied, and the more fully procedures and doctrine for using them have been assimilated, the better able will the forces be to conduct effective military operations within a toxic environment, and therefore the stronger will be the countermeasures that they provide. Civil defence measures may also be extended so as to provide antichemical protection for nonmilitary populations judged to be at special risk.

The route of deterrence seeks to pose a dissuasive counterthreat. That counterthreat may simply be one attribute of a general deterrent maintained against adversary aggression in any form. Or it may be conceived as a specific intra-war deterrent, aiming to dissuade adversary resort to CW even under circumstances where the general deterrent has failed to discourage adversary aggression. In neither case need the counterthreat take on a CW form, although, as we have seen, rationales have been developed in supportof in-kind counterthreats, especially for intra-war deterrence purposes.

Additionally or alternatively, there is the route of arms control. In its current form, a state can seek to join with others in an international collaboration that will eliminate chemical weapons and thus eradicate the threat altogether. In principle, the arms-control route offers the greatest enhancement of security, for unlike the other routes it can address the threat in all its varied aspects. In practice, it could offer security only if all the collaborating governments were to have enough confidence in the effectiveness of the implementing treaty to be able to resist internal pressures that would otherwise weaken or subvert the treaty regime. This in turn requires that those governments are sufficiently assured that their partners in the regime are also able and willing to resist such internal pressures. The procedures laid down by the treaty for verifying compliance are one of the means for generating assurance--for building confidence in the regime. There are others also.

In the present chapter we begin a closer study of this core problem of assurance, looking for general principles and then specific criteria that might be used to design the requisite provisions of the CWC. These provisions will institutionalize the procedures that are to give the international collaboration its necessary substance and the collaborating partners the confidence they need in order to make the regime work. Our starting point is an analysis of the detailed functions which the assurance provisions should serve.

In chapter 2 we began to formulate the problem in terms of the upper and lower bounds for the degree of assurance required. A perfectly effective regime would be one in which all participating states were in full compliance with the broad declaration of intention to which they had subscribed in the CWC. The desirable norm, we have seen, would take the form of preambular treaty language amounting to a renunciation of all activities intended to facilitate resort to chemical warfare. However, even if all states were in fact complying to this maximal degree, none of them could be fully confident that that was so, for intentions are not something whose absence can ever be confidently perceived. If, therefore, there can never be perfect assurance of full compliance, does this mean that the arms-control route is fundamentally flawed: that it is bound to be impossible to create a worthwhile CWC regime? Clearly not; or else the Geneva negotiations would not have been joined, let alone sustained for so long. Somewhere along the continuum ranging from zero to 100 per cent confidence in compliance, the negotiators, and therefore their instructing governments, evidently sense that an acceptable balance of risk and benefit can perhaps be struck.

The reason for this is of course that the defence and deterrence routes are themselves also flawed: antichemical protection can be overwhelmed or degrade the combat effectiveness of defence forces, deterrence may not work, and both may be vulnerable to technological surprise. So the choice for national CW policy is actually between national measures of self-reliance that afford less-than-perfect security against the CW threat and collaboration in a less-than-perfect international regime. Hence the formulation in chapter 2 that the degree of assurance required of the regime is that it should be sufficient to allow states to relax all those national measures they had adopted (or might be thinking of adopting) which would be incompatible with the regime, the scope of which they would themselves be defining. The quest is not for a perfect CWC regime; it is for a regime that offers a degree of security against the CW threat in all its aspects that is no worse, and preferably rather better, than that which is available from the national self-reliance routes alone. Such a regime would also reaffirm the moral values embodied in the existing anti-CW regime and would add to that common security derivable from any form of international collaboration.

Defining sufficiency here--deciding where along that zero to 100 per cent continuum benefit would begin to outweigh risk--will, as we have seen, be an essentially political matter for each participating state. But political though the ultimate choice may be, the range of options for it is nonetheless definable in security terms. For this task, several different rationales can no doubt be devised. The one we shall use is based on the guiding principle developed in chapter 2: that sufficiency may be determined from a comparison of the time that would be required to re-erect relaxed national measures with the warning time likely to be available of an adversary acting to take advantage of the relaxation.

On this approach we may specify the primary function of the rules and procedures laid down by the CWC in the following fashion: these provisions should have the effect of extending the warning time to the point where states parties would find acceptable the risk that they would not be able to re-adopt forgone countermeasures in time enough for them to serve their purpose. The procedures would thus be conceived of primarily as informational arrangements; the rules, as devices for ensuring the necessary quality and volume of information.

Historical experience suggests something of what the actual time periods dictating the sufficiency of the informational provisions might be. Elsewhere we review information on times taken to acquire various forms of offensive and defensive CW capability in US, British, French, German, Iraqi and Soviet programmes over the past seventy years. The guess might be hazarded from these data that a modern industrialized state, starting from scratch, could not reasonably expect to bring its armed forces to a significant state of protectedness against CW attack in much under five years, or to ready a supply of chemical weapons that would have military significance against protected enemy forces in less than one or two years. The most relevant point for us here is not what the actual numbers might be, for they will of course depend heavily on the prevailing circumstances, but rather that a full antichemical protective stance is likely to take substantially longer to acquire than a capability for using chemical weapons.

Provisions for assuring adequate warning

We can identify four broad ways in which the CWC regime could be designed and tuned through the provisions of the CWC itself so as to provide confidence in the sufficiency of warning time. We describe each in turn.

Information provisions

For any state, the task of securing the warning will fall, in the first instance, to its intelligence community. That community may or may not be a well-developed one. The estimates which it produces may or may not be competent or accurate. They may or may not be disseminated as rapidly as they could be. And they may or may not be given due notice by executive agencies of government. These are problems that lie outside our present concern. The point for us here is that it is in the available national CW-intelligence capacities that the prospects for an effective CWC regime are rooted.

One mechanism of increased assurance accordingly lies in incorporating into the regime a system for mutual information that would operate so that the CW-intelligence capacity of each of the collaborants in the regime became enhanced significantly, which is to say improved in one or both of two particular respects. The first would be an improvement which resulted in a general perception throughout government that the capacity had been increased and therefore that the warning time really was likely to be longer, or at least more reliable, with the CWC regime than without it. Note the presumption here that some form of CW-intelligence capacity already exists and will be retained throughout the CWC regime, even though it may consist of little more than some degree of access to the capacity of an allied country. It cannot be a function of the CWC to provide such a capacity *ab initio* to indigent states parties, nor, if it were, would any prudent government be likely to rely solely upon it. The second respect would be the improvement that would actually justify the perception of increased intelligence capacity, namely greater ability to discriminate between true and false signs of adversary noncompliance--for resolving ambiguities inherent in the available intelligence. Reference back to table 1 on page 19 illustrates the importance of such discrimination. Viewed from afar, many of the activities listed in the table could, as we have seen, appear to be serving more than one purpose. This means that there would be a certain risk, in the absence of the more detailed data that could be provided by the regime's information provisions, of mistaking permitted activities for illicit ones, and therefore of a false warning being uttered. It could also mean that illicit activities might be mistaken for permitted ones, so that an opportunity for early warning could be lost. All such activities we shall call 'ambiguous activities'.

In order to promote significantly the resolution of ambiguities, two categories of datum would need to enter the information pool. One category would comprise data about the nature of ambiguous permitted activities in progress. The other category would comprise data about CW programmes that had been continuing prior to the CWC and which had been discontinued in accordance with the treaty undertakings. The information provisions might accordingly include rules and procedures whereby states parties must declare to one another information from both these categories.

Capability-elimination provisions

The second pathway to confidence in the sufficiency of warning time is to incorporate within the regime rules that formally prohibit particular activities, and procedures that allow states parties to derive more assurance than their CW-intelligence capacities might otherwise be able to provide that others are acting in compliance with those rules. Such rules would, as we discuss further in chapter 6, be in addition to the general rules that are codified directly from the norm. The activities to be subjected to these special provisions might be of two broad types.

The first type comprises activities which, if they were to continue, would have the effect of obscuring warning signs. Such obfuscation might, for example, be the inadvertent consequence of some bona fide civil activity resembling an illicit one too closely for the two to be differentiated via the regime's information provisions and their associated national CW-intelligence capacities. That might be the case should a pesticide factory, say, decide to embark upon the production of a supertoxic new commodity. Or it might be the case if a new product required the creation of production capacity for an intermediate chemical whose only known utility hitherto was for CW-agent production. If the only way of preventing seriously damaging suspicions of noncompliance with the CWC from being generated by such ambiguous activities were to ban them--in these two examples, to outlaw all production of supertoxic pesticides and of particular CW-agent precursors, notwithstanding their civil applications--then maybe that is what the CWC should do, even though such activities had nothing directly to do with chemical weapons. For the present, it is by no means obvious that such Draconian measures would in fact be needed. It is a possibility which must, however, be recognized here.

The second broad type consists in those activities, all of them particular forms of ones listed in table 1, whose curtailment would greatly extend the time needed for a subsequent programme of illicit CW armament to be brought to security-threatening fruition, thereby extending the period within which warning could be obtained.

The value of CWC provisions along these two lines would largely depend on the intrinsic verifiability of the bans. It is this that sets the practical requirements for the procedures needed to provide verification of compliance [21]. There might be technical or political reasons why states parties would be unable to accept any of the procedures proposed, in which case nothing might be gained by having the rules at all. Worse, much might well be lost, for inadequately verifiable specific bans could become needless foci of dispute. It is a question of degree. Where intrinsic verifiability is relatively low, that could--if inclusion of the ban were nonetheless judged essential--be at least partly redressed by applying a multiplicity of verification procedures so as to amplify the assurance available from the ban [22].

Retained-countermeasure provisions

The third pathway is to narrow the scope of the CWC regime so that a significant range of national measures of self-reliance against the CW threat remain unconstrained by it. The more of these measures that can legitimately be retained, the smaller might the risk inherent in insufficient warning time appear to be (because some countermeasures would already be in place) and the shorter might be the warning time actually needed. However, just as such a limitation of scope could shorten the lead-time to acquisition of the full range of countermeasures, so also might it facilitate more rapid clandestine acquisition of a security-threatening offensive CW capability by an adversary state choosing to cheat the regime. Should that be the case the route could prove counterproductive, for it would reduce the period available for timely warning.

Yet this consideration points to one exemption from the scope of the CWC regime which, on our present conception, would in fact be essential for assurance: an exemption permitting activities associated with antichemical protection. We can see that if the latter were banned the period required for re-erection of relaxed countermeasures would almost certainly be considerably greater than the warning period for their need, simply because acquisition of good protection against chemical weapons is a much more time-consuming and resource-demanding process than acquisition of the weapons themselves. Such an exemption would unquestionably perpetuate several loci of ambiguity, not least because some degree of antichemical protection is also an essential component of offensive CW capability, but it should be possible to cope with them by suitable information and capability-elimination provisions. These are matters to which we shall return later.

For the moment let us simply give them the general label 'retained-countermeasure provisions'.

Also under this label comes national CW-intelligence capacity. But this is hardly an area in which international regulation is likely to serve much purpose, notwithstanding the central importance of such capacities for offensive CW capability no less than for the success of the CWC regime. In order to enhance the latter attribute, there might be point in including within the CWC an express ban on interference with 'national technical means'.

One further consideration having to do with retained countermeasures is the period of time that will actually be required for the elimination of national CW capabilities incompatible with the CWC. Rightly or wrongly, the view has taken hold in Geneva that 8 to 10 years will be needed for destruction of existing stockpiles of chemical weapons. This raises some intricate problems. Are states parties to rely solely on the Geneva Protocol for assurance that capabilities which have in effect been retained, albeit for purely practical reasons, will not be abused during the transitional period, or should they seek additional forms of assurance? Appearances are that there are no states today which possess significant quantities of chemical weapons which are not also parties to the Geneva Protocol; but appearances could be wrong. If the decision is not to have, say, international procedures for sealing or otherwise controlling stockpiles and production facilities upon entry-into-force of the CWC, should an ordering procedure be required for capability-elimination--rules specifying that production facilities should be eliminated ahead of stockpiles, for example, or that the most recently produced chemical weapons in the stockpile should be destroyed ahead of the older ones? Would such rules increase or diminish the assurance provided by the Geneva Protocol, having regard to the reservations of the right to retaliate in kind? At the very least, careful attention to the entry-into-force provisions of the CWC is required. They may perhaps need to ensure that chemical-weapons-possessor states do not find themselves compelled to conduct their elimination operations out of phase with one another.

Fallback provisions

The fourth pathway lies in the provision of special procedures which any state party may activate should it come to believe that events have invalidated its earlier perception of sufficient warning time. There are at least three such eventualities to which these fallback provisions might need to be responsive.

The first is perception of technical change having occurred of such a quality or magnitude that procedures then operating in accordance with the provisions just outlined might no longer be judged capable of providing adequate warning. The principal requirement here would seem to be that the CWC should include modernization provisions whereby information about pertinent technical change may be shared among states parties, and any amendments that might then be judged necessary may be made to the rules and procedures of the regime.

The second eventuality is that of a violation of the regime coming to be suspected by a state party, a violation having sufficient security-significance to generate pressure for withdrawal from the regime. The remedy here would be for the CWC to include challenge provisions whereby abnormal information requirements may be made of the suspected state party, with procedures capable of activation as necessary, including fact-finding procedures, for verifying or supplementing information resulting.

The third eventuality is that of the warning time having become demonstrably insufficient by virtue of an evident breach of the regime against which retained countermeasures would prove inadequate. In that dire emergency, withdrawal provisions should be available whereby an aggrieved state party might, if it chose, repudiate its CWC commitments without necessarily destroying the whole regime. The form which such provisions might take is not at all obvious, however. There might also be point in mutual-assistance provisions being written into the CWC whereby state parties undertake to give antichemical protective or remedial support to victims of actual CW attack.

Relative importance of the provisions

We may well conclude that, of these four pathways, it is the third, retained countermeasures, which, in its particular application to antichemical protection, has the greatest potential for promoting a successful CWC. The reason is twofold. The risks in subordination to a CWC regime which left antichemical protective activities untouched would be very much smaller than the risks in commitment to a perpetual vulnerability towards adversary cheating. Perhaps more important still, the retained antichemical-protection option would not require that national CW institutions be wound up. It would require, rather, that they be placed under tight surveillance. By incorporating retained-countermeasure provisions, the CWC regime would be exploiting in its favour the one major characteristic which sets chemical weapons apart from conventional and nuclear weapons: the fact that the target effects in most of the situations in which they might be used can be largely negated by feasible protective measures.

We noted above that problems would be created by exempting antichemical protective capability from the scope of the CWC. They would be difficult but surely not impossible to overcome. There would, in particular, be conflict with some of the capability-elimination provisions. That is because it is not possible to maintain a reliable anti-CW protective stance without investigating methods of CW attack. The exemption provisions would have to allow states parties the right to produce, for example, samples of supertoxic chemicals in order to assess the degree of threat they represented and the adequacy against them of existing protective countermeasures. The exemption provisions would also have to allow production of sample quantities of any chemical intermediates that could be used to synthesize potential CW agents, again for purposes of threat-assessment. So it would not be possible to place the total ban on production of especially ambiguous chemicals or their key precursors envisaged above as part of the capability-elimination provisions. Instead, there would have to be quantitative limits, and perhaps also a tight specification of where exactly the permitted production might take place. The international procedures that might be agreed for monitoring this permitted production in order to provide assurance that the exemption provisions were not being abused could also serve as the primary instrument for the requisite surveillance of national CW institutions.

Cheating

With these four broad possibilities in mind, let us now consider the requirements for assurance in their most extreme form.

The severest test of the CWC-regime's assurance provisions is their capacity for responding to fears that an adversary state may have chosen to submit itself to the regime, not because it wishes to bind itself to its undertakings and thereby promote CW disarmament, but in order to lull other states into a false sense of security and to provide itself with the option of taking advantage of their relaxation of countermeasures through a clandestine programme of CW armament; in short, cheating. Such a fear, implying belief in the readiness of governments to commit themselves to treaties of international law with which they had no intention of complying, would be a manifestation of the extremest form of mistrust between nations. It is nonetheless a real problem, for in any matter of confidence it is the perception, not the reality, that counts. Particular interest groups that feel themselves threatened by the projected Chemical Weapons

Convention may play upon this fear, and during periods of heightened international mistrust they can expect to gain substantial influence thereby.

On our warning time conception, such cheating would work only if the information procedures both of the regime and of the national intelligence communities concerned could be subverted into providing disinformation. We can see at once that the more procedures there are, each one yielding a different type of information, the lower would be the probability of any such deception succeeding; and the progression would be geometric, not arithmetic.

There is of course a presumption here that no clandestine programme of CW armament could ever be kept entirely secret. It is being supposed that, regardless of the security maintained around any such programme, the perturbations which it would be bound to cause within its immediate economic, social and natural environment would be discernible from afar if it really were being conducted on a significant scale--a presumption, in other words, that, if information about the programme is looked for in the right place and in the right manner, it will be found. Whether such an optimistic presumption is or is not correct is a matter for further research, for example by means of historical case studies set into due consideration of current information and surveillance technologies. The conclusion would almost certainly be that some of the requisite data-collection techniques would, by virtue of their cost or their technology, be available to only a very few states parties, as in the case of satellite-based imaging methods using advanced sensors. And it might also be that part of the requisite information would be derivable only through sources, technical or other, which the guardians of the clandestine programme would be able to destroy if their existence, and therefore information in any detail furnished by them, became more widely known. All of this would posit two requirements for the regime's information provisions. First, that they place an obligation upon states parties to disclose some specified types of information which would otherwise be available to other states parties only--if at all--through inaccessible sources or through ones liable to be compromised. Such disclosure could be achieved by an extension of the rules and procedures for declarations envisaged above. Second, that the information provisions include at least some capacity for verifying information furnished by states parties either about their own activities as disclosed in their obligatory declarations or about those of others. We will label what would be needed here 'information-verification procedures'.

In addition to these requirements of multiplicity, obligatory disclosure and at least some verification for the information provisions of the CWC, we can derive two other possibly useful design principles from the cheating problem. One is that confidence-building per se might take a place alongside warning-time assurance as an auxiliary function of the CWC procedures: the building of confidence, not so much in regime compliance (for that is the function of the information and capability-elimination provisions), but rather in the absence of regime-noncompliance. The aim of such confidence-building provisions would therefore be to furnish additional types of information serving, if not as actual evidence that states parties were not cheating, then at least as suggestive indication: a counterweight to the protestations of disaffected interest-groups seeking to exploit international mistrust. We shall return to this notion later; its weakness is that procedures based on it, if they did not also include information-verification procedures, could afford a hitherto unavailable conduit for projecting disinformation.

The other additional design-principle follows from the possibility, even the likelihood, that, if cheating by a state were to occur at all, it would be without the full sanction of government. It might instead take the form of a hidden or camouflaged programme to which access was controlled on a rigid need-to-know basis by whatever group was running it. That sponsoring agency would, however, require access to the national pool of materials and skills for the particular resources which its programme would need. It would therefore be liable to encounter the opposition of other agencies competing for those of the resources that were in short supply. Such opposition could be significantly strengthened were it to become known or suspected that the resources at issue were to be expended in a manner contrary to a national policy declaration--in this case, the duly ratified signature of the CWC by that state. Regime procedures which have the effect of familiarizing all spending departments and agencies of government with the particular types of resources needed to prosecute an illicit CW programme could therefore also have the effect of forcing a decision on the future of that programme up to the highest levels of government: to a level, in other words, where a much wider range of costs, especially political ones, would enter into consideration than before. The requirement for this to work would not only be that information about requisite resources were made available under the information provisions. Much more important would be that those provisions required all states parties to create a sufficiently representative national control organ tasked with domestic implementation of the CWC; an organ which would receive all information generated from the assurance procedures.

Against cheating under full governmental authority, the feasible safeguards are bound to be flawed, for their central element, the challenge procedures of the CWC fallback provisions, can operate only by, in effect, requiring the cheater to disclose incriminating information.

So it is this consideration which represents the acid test of CW arms control. The national self-reliance options for CW policy cannot surmount the risk that CW deterrence may fail, or that CW defences may be overwhelmed. The arms-control option cannot entirely forfend the risk of adversary cheating. The choice between the policy options is a choice between risks. Interest-groups opposed to the CWC can, as we have noted, be expected to extol the dangers inherent in adversary cheating simply because there is no complete remedy for it. Yet, although neither the possibility of cheating nor its dangers can be gainsaid, they must be kept in proportion. On any rational calculus, the probability of CWC-cheating must surely be judged low, if only because the benefits to be gained from a clandestine capability in weapons of limited military value would themselves be low. And those benefits would be diminished by the option which, on the retained-countermeasure approach outlined above, would remain open to all states parties to maintain anti-CW protective capability.

The cheating problem, we may conclude, is more a political than a substantive impediment to CW arms control. No doubt a degree of cynicism towards the real intentions of negotiating governments is prudent, and to that extent the problem is a cause for concern. But the real and much more serious risk to security is surely not premeditated cheating. It lies rather in the dual dangers of misperception--of incentives to violate CWC-undertakings being generated from misinterpretation of ambiguous data--and of intentions changing under the lure of some newly opened opportunity.

Projecting assurance

The foundation of a strategy for assurance against these more tenuous dangers exists in adoption of some or all of the different sets of CWC provisions thus far suggested by our application of the warning-time principle. Let us now consider whether any further elements are needed.

Looking at the sorts of procedural and legal arrangements that would be involved in institutionalizing those various provisions, we can see that there is another distinction that can be drawn and usefully developed further. There are, on the one hand, those arrangements which an individual state party may use in order to derive the assurance that it needs of adequate warning time. On the other hand, there are the arrangements which it may use in order to facilitate the acquisition of such assurance by other states parties so that the latter will not, because they lack adequate assurance, take steps which might endanger its own security by endangering the regime. This is a distinction between getting something out of the regime and putting something into it. Clearly, some of the provisions must be designed so as to be usable in both ways, above all the information provisions. Others, for example any confidence-building provisions that may be thought worthwhile in the light of the cheating problem, might serve the regime best if designed primarily for assurance-projection rather than assurance-acquisition.

Our emphasis thus far has been upon the latter because we have formulated the basic requirement of assurance in terms of the ability of a participating government to resist domestic pressures either for rejection of the projected CWC regime or, later on, for repudiation of the treaty or subversion of the regime by clandestine rearmament. But of course the regime will only work if, like any other bargain, there is both give and take.

We thus arrive at one final design-requirement for the assurance strategy: that it should facilitate the giving as well as the receiving of assurance.

Two broad ways can be identified in which assurance may be projected. One way is for a state to make information about its own affairs available to others, information of types such as we have already considered, and verifiable if necessary. The other way is for a state to engage in, and be seen to be engaging in, positively reassuring activities: publicly destroying any stocks of chemical weapons or production capacity for them which it may have, for example, and otherwise acting in a fashion clearly demonstrating that it is dismantling all elements of its CW capability that are incompatible with the CWC. It seems important that, for both options, the CWC should make provision for procedures that facilitate such displays.

To this end, the capability-elimination provisions considered earlier might be extended so as to place verified bans, not just on those activities that could increase the rate of acquisition of security-threatening capability, but on any form of proscribed capability whose elimination would have an amenable degree of intrinsic verifiability. To increase the flow of assuring information, specially facilitating rules might be incorporated within the regime.

Rules obliging states parties to declare information or to provide it upon challenge can go only a part of the way towards this latter objective, for some of the information required for the smooth running of the regime will be of so sensitive a character as to discourage candour even when its disclosure is mandatory, let alone voluntary. The remedy would seem to lie in incorporating safeguards into the information provisions whose effect would be to reduce the risks and costs of disclosure. To see what these safeguards might be let us review the main types of information whose pooling has thus far appeared desirable, giving particular examples of each.

(1) About ambiguous contiguous activities. Information otherwise private to, or unavailable beyond the borders of, each participating country about any of its activities which, although having nothing whatever to do with CW capability, have a close enough resemblance to be liable to be confused with illicit activities. The primary examples are industrial activities involving 'dual-purpose' chemicals, ones which either are potential CW agents or could be used to produce them, as well as being industrial commodities or intermediates. An example of information of this type would be an annual return detailing the production and consumption of, say, hydrogen cyanide (a dual-purpose CW agent) or methylphosphonyl dichloride (a dual-purpose precursor) at a a particular factory.

(2) About ambiguous permitted activities. Information likewise unavailable internationally about activities that are proceeding within participating countries for permitted purposes in the sense of the retained-countermeasure provisions (or, more generally, according to the sense in

which 'chemical weapons' are defined in the CWC) but which, again, are liable to be confused with illicit activities. Examples would include research and development programmes in the field of antichemical protection involving the production of the substantial quantities of actual CW agent that might be required for testing purposes. Accordingly, an example of this information-type would be an annual return of the total quantity of, say, a nerve gas produced in a country, with particulars of where it had been made and what had been done with it.

(3) About renounced prior activities. Information of a type that would have been held secret prior to the CWC about activities forgone under the terms of the treaty and about renounced CW capabilities. The primary examples are size and composition of chemical-weapons stockpiles and locations of production and storage facilities.

(4) About resources needed for chemical weapons. Information identifying the resources needed to acquire illicit CW capability, especially the skills and the particular chemicals needed to manufacture CW agents. An example would be a list of the chemical precursors that would go into the production of a particular CW agent, candidate or actual.

(5) About pertinent scientific and technical developments. Information identifying particular scientific discoveries or other developments that bear upon the purposes of the CWC, especially information suggestive of a newly emergent threat to the effectiveness of antichemical protection.

The five information categories, let us recall, have been posited as the central elements on which an assurance strategy might be based. Our working hypothesis has been that, if states parties were to agree to pool sufficient information from within each of the categories, much of the basis would thereby be created for confidence in the adequacy of warning time. Over and above this, a further form of information-flow has also been envisaged in the assurance strategy, namely that involved in certain specific forms of verification also required by one or another of the projected pathways to assured warning time. Our analysis thus far has suggested roles for two broad types: information-verification, namely the validation of certain types of pooled information, including information furnished under challenge provisions; and compliance-verification, whereby compliance with particular rules requiring certain capability-eliminations is ascertained. The actual verification procedures used will inevitably involve the disclosure of yet more information, some of which may be sensitive. For example, techniques of on-site, near-site or off-site inspection, with or without complementary use of remotely controlled sealed instrumentation, might prove to be the best way of achieving some forms of compliance- or information-verification; in which case everything observable by such inspection would, at least in theory, enter the total pool of shared information.

Finally there are the requirements, such as they might be, for the pooling of information as confidence-building measures: any additional types of information of which disclosure would promote assurance of the absence of noncompliance with the CWC regime. The primary example would be information about current research, development, training and deployment activities associated with antichemical protection.

The disadvantages and dangers that might attend disclosure would take on different aspects for each of the various information-categories, and would affect states parties at different levels. Some disclosures might endanger the regime as a whole; some might harm some states parties but not others; some might penalize some interest-groups to the benefit of their competitors. For example, as regards categories (3), (4) and (5), information released might facilitate CW armament programmes in countries outside the CWC regime, or might actively stimulate countries within it to reconsider their commitment to the regime in the light of new

CW-armament options thereby revealed. This might seem a relatively minor risk in the case of categories (3) and (4), since so much of that information is in the public domain already; but it could conceivably become a major problem as regards category (5). Again, with respect to all categories other than (3) and (4), there is the possibility that disclosure could be exploited by other states parties or by commercial interests to acquire valuable proprietary or otherwise legitimately confidential information not germane to assurance requirements. This risk might become particularly acute in the case of site inspections at manufacturing facilities.

There is, furthermore, always the risk that the more information that is made available, the more may be expected or demanded, perhaps even to the point where failure for quite proper reasons to provide it becomes a source of mistrust and damaging dispute between states parties. This could become a major problem in circumstances when, for one reason or another, many activities were expressly exempted from the scope of the regime. It could also confound challenge procedures. There, it would be one aspect of a more general design problem: that of ensuring that when disputes between states parties about compliance do arise, neither side to the dispute is discouraged from participating in its resolution--nor, conversely, encouraged to impede resolution--by the machinery which the regime provides for that purpose being either inequitable or ill-prepared or simply nonexistent.

The safeguards and remedies needed to loosen all these and other inhibitions affecting information-disclosure for assurance-projection must lie in the actual mechanics of disclosure: in how the international pooling of information is in fact to be done, who precisely is to get the information, what degrees of confidentiality are to be maintained, who is to define the types of information that are to be subject to mandatory disclosure, and so on. We can thus see that the details of the organizational arrangements that are to underpin the CWC regime may be critical to the degree of assurance derivable by states parties, and therefore critical to the success both of the negotiations and then of the treaty. The overarching organizational device must probably be a Consultative Committee of States Parties. We shall not venture here into any detailed consideration of what its powers, functions and subsidiary organs should be, nor of the nature of the preparatory commission that should pave the way towards it during the period between signature and entry into force of the CWC. We will note only the heavy weight of responsibility that will fall upon it.

The range of assurance provisions needed

We may now see that there is a wide variety of conceivable assurance provisions from amongst which it may be possible to arrive at consensus on one particular set of rules and procedures which together would comprise the core of the CWC regime. So, returning to our basic framework of analysis as we left it at the end of chapter 2, we are now able to begin introducing into it a detailed array of suboptions for policy on either side of the projected barter: we can visualize from application of the warning-time principle the actual ways in which individual states parties could derive sufficient assurance of compliance on the part of antagonistic states for the exchange of the national self-reliance basket for the international collaboration basket to become an attractive proposition: to make them better off inside the CWC regime than outside it.

We can also be more specific about what is meant by 'sufficient' assurance. It means, in our analysis, assurance great enough for the government of the state in question to be able to resist any internal pressure there may be for abrogation under all circumstances where adversaries are not in fact violating the regime on a scale or at a rate great enough to pose a real danger of retained or acquirable countermeasures proving inadequate.

Sufficiency in this sense is thus a function not only of the regime itself, but also of intragovernmental politics. A projected regime which was judged sufficient by one government might be judged insufficient by another even when the states that they both govern are subject to an identical CW menace. By precisely the same token, a particular set of assurance arrangements proposed for the CWC that would otherwise be judged sufficient after conclusion of the treaty might be judged unacceptable during the negotiations and therefore rejected. For after a government has concluded a treaty, the weight of opinion seeing value in the treaty is bound to increase, at least in the short term. An agreement on something as peripheral as chemical warfare seems unlikely to become a national issue on the scale of, say, SALT II in US politics. The case that must then be made in order to create widespread intragovernmental doubt about the worth of the treaty--the case, that is to say, for disturbing a formalized status quo in which leading figures have invested prestige--must therefore become correspondingly stronger.

While institutional factors may then be operating in favour of the treaty, it is also conceivable that they might be operating to sustain a delusion: to promote assurance which the actual behaviour of other states does not warrant. That risk gives especial force to the arguments of those who, during the negotiations, see inadequacy in the verification and other arrangements proposed to satisfy the assurance function. Yet that in turn creates a risk that those arguments may lend protective cover to interests whose opposition to the arrangements has nothing whatever to do with the capacity of the arrangements for disclosing adversary noncompliance. This is a risk that becomes particularly damaging to the prospects for a CWC in cases where interest groups that seek to use this protective cover to dissemble their fundamental opposition to any form of CWC are also seen by their respective governments as the principal source of expertise on what is necessary in the way of verification.

All of which lends further emphasis, if that were needed, to the central theme of our analysis: that the manner in which assurance provisions are ultimately chosen for inclusion in CWC drafts requires particularly circumspect attention, in full recognition that matters of great sensitivity and delicacy are involved.

Chapter 6. Rules and procedures of the projected treaty regime

Our analysis suggests, then, that the value of the CWC could be assured by incorporating four main categories of treaty provision, their operation to be overseen by a suitably constituted Consultative Committee.

The four main categories were: retained-countermeasure provisions, capability-elimination provisions, information provisions, and fallback provisions (including challenge, modernization, withdrawal and mutual-assistance provisions).

As envisaged in chapter 5, these categories and their various subcategories were elastic enough to comprise a rather wide range of elements, some of which were exemplified, others not. Several of these elements are clearly going to be essential if the purpose of the treaty--precluding chemical warfare--is to be implemented. Others may appear less important when our analytical framework is completed, even unnecessary. Which is which we cannot begin to judge without moving further away from the general to the particular--without considering in some detail the specifics that must direct the actual rules and procedures comprising the projected international collaboration. This we shall now do.

Our aim is a synopsis whereby all the rules and procedures that might constitute the overall CWC regime may be seen both in relation to one another and to the precise purposes which they would serve. Such a synopsis, which is presented in table 4 at the end of this chapter, should allow us to recognize more easily than would otherwise be the case which are the more important and which are the less important aspects of the projected regime. We should then be able to specify more clearly the negotiating options: the degrees of freedom within the total system whereby particular interests may be accommodated with minimal detriment either to themselves or to the projected regime.

Function into form

It is from function, not form, that our categories and subcategories of assurance provision have thus far been defined. The form which each must take in the CWC itself can be seen to comprise one or more of four basic types of treaty-element:

Normative rules, codified directly from the agreed basic norm, whereby states parties commit themselves either to do something or to refrain from doing something else--'positive obligations' or 'negative obligations'--and whereby the scope of the regime is defined.

Prescriptions of procedures, required to implement the purpose of the CWC, whereby states parties agree to conduct business with one another on particular matters in particular ways. These prescriptions might appear in annexes or protocols to the CWC, in accordance with general principles and criteria enunciated in the treaty itself.

Procedural rules, also codified as either positive or negative obligations, whereby the procedures required to implement the purpose of the CWC are established, standardized to the extent necessary for their smooth operation, and otherwise regulated so as to provide states parties with maximal assurance of general compliance with the normative rules.

Definitions, whereby states parties record their common understanding of those particular terms used in the codification of rules on which consensus is essential for the effective operation of the prescribed procedures.

The normative rules and associated definitions

It might in theory be possible to limit the normative rules to a single rule that simply restates the basic norm (discussed in chapter 2) as a negative obligation. It might take some such form as the following:

> Each Party undertakes neither to conduct any activities in preparation for use of chemical weapons nor to assist anyone else to do so.

A definition of 'chemical weapons' would be associated with it.

However, there is now general consensus in Geneva that more specificity is needed, in two respects. First, at least some of the actual activities that are to be forgone should be specified, as by means of a formula whereby states parties undertake not to develop, produce, otherwise acquire, stockpile or retain chemical weapons, or transfer them to anyone. Second, the negative obligations to refrain from producing and retaining chemical weapons which would be contained in such a formula should be supplemented by positive obligations to destroy any weapons possessed and to eliminate any production facilities for them. In addition, and notwithstanding the existence of the Geneva Protocol, there is also concern that the basic purpose of the CWC should be reflected in a rule committing states parties to abstain from actual use of chemical weapons. Beyond this, it is now generally agreed in Geneva that the CWC should, in order to facilitate implementation, provide for procedures of consultation and co-operation mediated through a Consultative Committee of states parties.

We may take that consensus as our point of departure. Let us begin with the matter of the definitions that need to be associated with it, in particular the crucial definition of 'chemical weapon'.

The definition of chemical weapons

At the beginning of chapter 4, we used a target-effects criterion to differentiate chemical weapons from other categories, contrasting the physical destruction available from the sources of thermal or kinetic energy used in conventional weapons with the biospecific damage available from toxicity. This certainly reflects the consensus in Geneva that chemical weapons, in the sense of the CWC, should not subsume incendiary weapons, even though the latter are weapons whose effects depend upon the properties of particular chemicals, any more than they should subsume high-explosive weapons, which also rely on particular chemical properties. The requirement clearly is for a definition that rests on the particular property of poisonousness--of toxicity.

But toxicity to what: to people only, or any other type of conceivable target to which biospecific damage might aid the attacking forces--livestock, food-crops, natural cover, and such like? It is primarily as regards herbicide warfare that this is a contentious issue. The considerations in the concluding section of chapter 4 point strongly towards an extensive rather than a limited approach here: of including, not excluding, toxicity towards plant life within the operative criterion.

Then there is the question of type and degree of toxicity. Are we talking only of lethal toxicity or of toxicity more generally defined to subsume any form of harm to a living organism; and are we talking only of permanent harm, which is the common connotation of 'poison', or of both permanent and transient harm, as in the normal technical sense of 'toxic'? Clearly we should not be considering only lethal toxicity, for the military utility of substances such as mustard gas is by no means dependent upon the mortal hazards they can create. But if deadly poisonousness is not to be the criterion, is it possible to draw any sort of line at all? All substances are harmful to living organisms if the dosage is high enough and can be permanently so. It is primarily as regards tear gas that this is a contentious matter. Again, the considerations at the end of chapter 4 point to an inclusive rather than an exclusive definition. The precise mechanism of the toxicity may also be relevant if the aim is to create a clear demarcation between chemical weapons on the one hand and radiological or biological weapons on the other.

Finally there is the question: toxicity of what? If the operative criterion is to speak of toxic chemicals, then what is a 'chemical'? Is it only something whose intimate structure is definable in terms of the formulae which a particular group of people--chemists--use to encapsulate observations? Is it only something that can be replicated by procedures those same people have developed, the procedures of chemical synthesis? These are the ways most dictionaries define the term. But in either case, what of the many poisons that have been isolated from the natural world, but whose identity has not yet been defined in precise chemical formulae, and which have not yet been replicated by chemical synthesis? All such substances are 'toxins' in the sense in which that term is used in the 1972 Biological Weapons Convention, so their development, production and stockpiling for weapons purposes is already outlawed. But there are many toxins whose chemical structure is known and which can be synthesized by chemists: does this mean that they should be included in or excluded from the scope of the CWC? Since there is at least one toxin within the meaning of the Biological Weapons Convention that is also a standard CW agent--hydrogen cyanide--some overlap is going to have to be accepted. Should not all toxins, then, be subsumed within the CWC, thereby bringing all poisons, whether natural or synthetic, within the scope of the assurance provisions of the CWC? There seems to be no good reason for not doing so. In that case it had better be 'toxic substance' or 'toxic agent', not 'toxic chemical', that is used in the definition of chemical weapon.

A toxic substance <u>per se</u> is not a weapon: it has somehow to be delivered to its target. Yet it is possible to conceive of combat situations in which the simplest of delivery means would suffice, even improvised ones, and others in which toxic substances could have aggressive value only if highly specialized delivery means were available. The operative definition would therefore have to cover both together and separately toxic substances and means specifically designed for their delivery. Nor would that be sufficient. Munitions are now becoming available for standard delivery systems which, although designed to achieve their target effects through toxicity, are not actually loaded with the toxic agent whereby those effects are achievable. They are instead loaded with separate canisters of chemicals, not especially toxic ones, which are adapted to mix together and create the toxic agent by chemical reaction only during the brief period immediately prior to coincidence of target and munition--while the bomb is falling or the artillery-shell is on its target-trajectory. These are the so-called 'binary' munitions. The operative definition must therefore extend to the individual chemical reactants that constitute the precursors of the toxic agent which such munitions generate. Nor even might this be sufficient, for there are other ways too in which a mixture of chemicals may exert more pronounced toxic effects than any one component of the mixture alone. There may be synergism in their toxic action. Or one of the chemicals might act as a carrier for another, or have the effect of breaching antichemical protective measures that would otherwise be effective against highly toxic components of the mixture. Taking all such adjuvants as well as precursors into account, we can see that the operative definition may need to cover a rather wide variety of chemicals that do not themselves have pronounced toxic effects.

Yet another complication exists in the usefulness, to which we have already referred, of many toxic substances, including some standard CW agents, for purposes having nothing to do with CW: as drugs, as biocides for use against animal- or insect-pests or against weeds, as industrial intermediates, and so on. The same is true for the majority of precursors. Tear gases, too, are dual purpose in this sense, finding application in the hands of domestic police forces. The operative definition must not only, we can therefore see, embrace a very wide range of different materials; it must also exempt many of those materials in their application for non-CW purposes.

It cannot yet be said that any fully satisfactory definition of chemical weapons has yet found consensus in Geneva. The task, however, is not an impossible one, and will surely be speedily discharged as soon as the basically political problem of the degree of proscription that is to be applied under the CWC to tear gases, herbicides and toxins has been resolved. The facilitating breakthrough came several years ago with the gradual display of agreement on an approach which said, in effect, that any toxic substance which was not specifically intended for some non-CW purpose should fall within the scope of the treaty, regardless of its actual utility in CW. What has thus come to be known as the 'general purpose criterion' is being applied in all the current attempts at finding an acceptable definition by defining chemical weapons so as to include all toxic agents/chemicals "except those intended for permitted purposes". The great advantage of this approach, as opposed to one in which the definition rests on, say, the concept of chemical warfare itself (as by defining 'CW agents'), is that it is forward-looking: it will not lock the CWC into 1980s-conceptions of how CW may be conducted.

Subsidiary definitions: correlating levels of risk and control

Use of the general purpose criterion requires that a definition of 'permitted purposes' takes its place alongside the other subordinate definitions which we have just seen will also be required, in particular a definition of 'precursor', and perhaps 'adjuvant', too. Some permitted purposes may involve toxic chemicals or their precursors being developed, produced, otherwise acquired, stockpiled, retained or transferred on a substantial scale, thereby presenting an ambiguous appearance to outsiders uninformed about the true nature of those purposes, and so creating some of the problems of assurance addressed in chapter 5. Other such permitted purposes might create production capacity for CW-agent precursors which would not otherwise exist, precursors that might be used either in binary munitions or in plant-process production. Several more such ambiguities can be envisaged, varying in their degree of severity. Just as CW agents may be ranked according to the degree of threat they pose (as we saw in chapter 4), so too may ambiguities associated with chemicals involved in permitted purposes be ranked according to the importance for assurance purposes of their being clarified. It follows, therefore, that a third tier of definitions is also going to be required: definitions that differentiate categories both of toxic agent and of precursor--and maybe even of adjuvant, too--according to the level of control that ought to be applied to them.

Without good third-tier definitions, national CWC-implementation authorities would have difficulty in determining what degree of supervision they were expected to apply to individual chemical facilities in their own countries. And manufacturing enterprises in the chemical industry would not know whether this or that chemical whose production they were contemplating was or was not liable to governmental regulation in accordance with CWC undertakings. The pressure of domestic interests, to say nothing of bureaucratic inertia, would be likely to promote less rather than more regulation. In the absence of clear third-tier definitions, then, the background against which the CWC assurance provisions would be operating might be dangerously confusing.

In table 3 below, seventeen classes of CW-relevant chemical are differentiated and exemplified, each class presenting a distinctive control problem. Within each class there will be chemicals that have a greater or a lesser degree of importance from the standpoint of assurance, the variation reflecting their relative attractiveness for CW-purposes--the degree of threat they might represent either if stockpiled as fill for chemical munitions, binary or nonbinary, or as feedstock for CW-agent factories. This threat-ranking concept is illustrated in the table by assigning the specific examples given for each class of chemical to one or another of four threat-levels according to (unstated) criteria common to all seventeen classes: high (threat-level 1), medium (threat-level 2), low (threat-level 3) and negligible (threat-level 4).

Table 3. Exemplified classes of chemical having different significances for the CWC regime

Class of chemical	Specific examples, at threat-level 1	2	3	4
SINGLE PURPOSE CHEMICALS				
A Toxic chemicals whose only utility, other than for research or protective purposes, is as CW agents	Soman	.	.	.
	Mustard	.	.	.
	.	3-Quinuclidinyl benzilate		
	.	.	Lewisite	.
B Chemicals whose only utility, other than for research or protective purposes, is as precursors for loading binary munitions	Methylphosphonyl difluoride			.
	.	Pinacolyl alcohol		.
C Chemicals whose only utility, other than for research or protective purposes, is as loadings for multicomponent chemical weapons other than binary munitions	.	.	Certain fluorocarbons	
	.	.	.	Chlorine trifluoride
D Chemicals whose only utility, other than for research or protective purposes, is as precursors for plant-process production of CW agents	.	.	1-Methyl-4-piperidinol	
DUAL PURPOSE CHEMICALS				
E Toxic chemicals once used or stockpiled as CW agents which are also civilian commodities in large-scale production*	.	Certain herbicides		.
	.	Phosgene	.	.
	.	Hydrogen cyanide		.
	.	.	Cyanogen chloride	
	.	.	Chloropicrin	
	.	.	Chlorine	.
F Toxic chemicals once used or stockpiled as CW agents which are also civilian commodities in small-scale production*	.	Certain tear gases		.
	.	Certain toxins (as used for toxoid production)		
G Toxic chemicals that are civilian commodities which, in view of the scale on which they are available, might be considered as candidate CW agents	.	.	Tetraethyl lead	
H Toxic chemicals that have in the past had sizeable civil applications	.	Amiton	.	.
I Toxic chemicals that are civilian commodities which have toxic properties conducive to CW purposes but for which purposes the available production capacity is too limited	.	Certain veterinary drugs		
	.	Certain other drugs (e.g., LSD)		
	.	.	Certain mammalian-pest killers	
J Toxic chemicals that are produced on a substantial scale for military applications only, but ones unrelated to CW	.	.	Certain rocket propellants	
K Chemicals that are civilian commodities which are also CW-agent precursors suitable for loading binary munitions	.	Certain alcohols		.
	.	Sulphur	.	.
	.	.	Thiodiglycol	

Class of chemical	Specific examples, at threat-level 1	2	3	4
L Chemicals that are civilian commodities which also have candidacy as loadings for multicomponent weapons other than binary munitions	. .	. .	. .	Dimethyl sulphoxide Certain furans
M Chemicals that are civilian commodities in large-scale production* which could also be used as precursors in plant-process production of CW agents or their immediate precursors	. .	. .	Phosphorus trichloride Phosphoryl chloride	
N The same as M, but in only limited production	. .	Methylphosphonyl dichloride Dimethyl methylphosphonate		
O Chemicals that are produced on a substantial scale for military applications unrelated to CW as well as for civilian applications and which could also be used as precursors in plant-process production of CW agents or their precursors	.	.	Elemental phosphorus	
P Chemicals, including future ones, having large-scale potential as civilian commodities which, if that potential were realized, could induce large-scale production* of intermediates which could also be used as precursors of CW agents	.	Methylphosphonate or ethylphosphonate pesticides, herbicides and c.		
Q Chemicals produced on a large scale* for civilian purposes in chemical-process plant that could also be used to produce CW agents or binary precursors of them	.	.	Probably a great many	

* The difference implied here between large-scale and small-scale production is that the former involves production capacity easily large enough to support supply of the chemicals in question on a scale sufficient for significant CW purposes.

The concept embodied in the general purpose criterion is that <u>all</u> chemicals should fall within the scope of the CWC, but that the terms of the CWC should not inhibit any use of them for 'permitted purposes'. If we now apply the concept to the analysis of assurance requirements presented in chapter 5, we see that the latter in fact envisages five different levels of control to which any one particular chemical might be subject under the CWC regime:

<u>Control-level 1</u>. The chemical is banned for all purposes except protective purposes. Information on quantities stockpiled for CW purposes at the time of entry into force of the CWC to be declared, together with information about production capacity, such declarations to be subject to verification procedures. Production for protective purposes to be subject to strict controls, including quantitative limits and reporting requirements. Nonproduction for purposes other than protective purposes to be verified.

<u>Control-level 2</u>. The chemical is banned except for permitted purposes. Information on quantities produced and consumed for permitted purposes to be declared, the declarations to be subject to verification procedures.

<u>Control-level 3</u>. The chemical is banned except for permitted purposes. Information on quantities produced and consumed for permitted purposes to be declared, but not subject to verification procedures.

<u>Control-level 4</u>. The chemical is banned except for permitted purposes. No other provisions.

<u>Control-level 5</u>. Applicable to newly discovered chemicals or to known chemicals having newly discovered properties which have a CW significance of a kind that ought to be considered under the CWC review provisions. The chemical is banned except for permitted purposes. An onus exists upon any government becoming aware of such chemicals to declare information facilitating the CWC review procedure.

The obvious logic, then, is that chemicals at a high threat-level in the sense of table 3 should be subject to a high control-level as just outlined, while those at lower threat-levels should be subject to lower control-levels. That would, however, be a counsel of perfection, for if one looks more closely at the nature of each of the 17 classes in table 3, it can at once be seen that several considerations of practical feasibility are likely to prevent this. For example, where the level of production of a chemical for civil purposes is large and its end-uses numerous, the prospects for verifying declared information about production and consumption--that is, for achieving some assurance of nondiversion for CW purposes--are likely to be poor. In that case, assignment of the chemical to a control-level requiring such verification might be pointless--unless states parties were prepared to put a lot of manpower and regulatory effort into the control. Or there might be instances where legitimate secrecy precluded sufficient declaration, in which case assignment to a lower control-level, one that did not require declaration might be unavoidable--unless states parties were to waive the secrecy by compelling their industrial enterprises to disclose proprietary information or by relaxing the security maintained around military information.

Concordance of threat-level and control-level is, we can thus see, a delicate area for negotiation. It is one of two or three areas where factional interests are likely to have a directing influence on the final shape of the CWC. On the surface, the matter of the third tier of definitions may appear as a largely formal problem. Underneath, it is in fact a substantive problem of central significance to the long-term value of the CWC regime.

Toxicity criteria and their limitations

Progress thus far towards the resolution of the problem is principally to be seen in the emergence of a general consensus that toxicity criteria should be used to differentiate chemicals for control purposes. Further, there is general agreement on a quantitative specification of two thresholds of toxicity, and active debate on a third threshold as well. Two thresholds mean that three classes of chemical are being defined; three thresholds, four classes. The choice of toxicity as the criterion for differentiation implies correlation of control-level and threat-level. The fact that toxicity criteria are inapplicable to the threats presented by adjuvants and precursors is, of course, recognized. As regards precursors, there is consensus on the need for a threshold that would isolate 'key precursors', and a debate on additional thresholds is beginning. The operative criterion to be used for differentiation of precursors remains unresolved. As regards adjuvants, the problem--if in fact it is here a real one in security terms--has scarcely been addressed.

Ideally the thresholds chosen to differentiate control-levels would be definable on general criteria, which is to say applicable even to substances as yet unrecognized or undiscovered. For precursors and adjuvants, it is unlikely that any such general criterion will be found, in which case the problem may prove resolvable only through the use of lists of specific chemicals. Such an approach would place a major burden on the CWC review machinery. Even for the toxic agents themselves, a listing approach may also prove necessary to supplement the toxicity criteria. This is because there are some forms of toxicity which cannot yet be measured in ways simple or reproducible enough for thresholds between control-levels to be specified with sufficient sharpness for the purposes of the CWC regime. Acute lethal toxicity is relatively easy to quantify in a treaty-sufficient manner, as is reflected in the language that has already found consensus in Geneva--language differentiating 'supertoxic lethal', 'other lethal' and 'other harmful' chemicals according to a prescribed procedure for measuring acute-LD50s in laboratory animals. But this is not so for forms of toxicity that do not manifest themselves primarily in death--forms that are exploited in incapacitating chemical weapons based on, for example, supertoxic psychotropic agents or tear gases. Nor is it so for the many forms of non-acute toxicity as displayed by, for example, carcinogenic or mutagenic agents. As CW is currently conceived, toxicity criteria relying on measurement of acute lethality are probably just about sufficient for capturing, and therefore bringing under control, all those chemical weapons which states currently perceive as the principal threats. Yet should it happen that a much greater degree of military interest than exists at present were to build up in, say, genetic, carcinogenic or psychotropic weapons, a CWC regime structured according to acute lethal toxicity criteria could prove seriously inadequate. By that time, perhaps, scientific inquiry might have provided the technical basis, currently lacking, for further criteria. But if that were thought unlikely, the remedy might be to abandon toxicity criteria altogether and rely solely on listing according to perceived-risk criteria. The CWC could be a lot simpler and therefore more manageable if agents, adjuvants and precursors were all treated in a similar fashion. The general purpose criterion would remain in place to capture unlisted CW agents.

The procedural rules and prescribed procedures

The notion of correlating degrees of threat with degrees of control allows us to proceed straight into the synoptic overview of what the CWC may need to comprise overall. It allows us to transform our four categories of function-defined treaty provision into sets of treaty-elements. Thus, we are now able to analyse those four categories in terms of the international procedures that the treaty may need to provide, the procedural rules that it may need to codify, and the definitions it may need to elaborate in order that sufficient assurance be created among states parties that they are indeed all conforming with the basic norm.

Such an analysis is presented in table 4. The entries in the 'procedures', 'rules' and 'definitions' column are purely illustrational and are not meant to represent all the possibilities. They are given solely in order to exemplify the sorts of formal provision that might be needed in order to effect the assurance function concerned. Some of the examples may well, when our overall analytical framework is complete, appear either deficient or excessive or unnecessary or imprudent.

The entries in the 'definitions' column have deliberately been left in a crude form. Obviously there can be no place in an international treaty for language as subjective as that which is used in the table to differentiate chemical threat-levels and thereby to allocate control-levels: "especially threatening", "CW agent", "major dual-purpose chemicals" and "particularly ambivalent chemicals". The language has been left that way to serve as a reminder of the caveat entered earlier in this chapter: that, although the matter of definitions may appear on the surface to be no more than a formal problem, it is in fact a crucial area of negotiation, one in which the subordination of factional interests to the greater good is likely to be fought with particular intensity.

Table 4. Exemplified types of treaty-element required for the assurance provisions

ovision for assuring CWC value, fined by function	Requisite international procedure	Requisite rule	Requisite definitions
e basic norm, setting the scope of the CWC	1 Procedure for consultation and co-operation in any matter related to implementation	1 Ban on production, development and use of chemical weapons and on any other activities associated with them (cp. table 1) not for specified permitted purposes 2 Obligation to participate in a Consultative Committee having a specified composition and mandate	'Chemical weapons' 'Permitted purposes'
ne retained-countermeasure provisions: To reduce risks inherent in imperfect assurance of compliance by permitting retention of some measures of national self-reliance, including: -- antichemical protection			'Protective purposes' to be specified among the 'permitted purposes'
-- undiminished CW-intelligence capacity		3 Ban on interference with (legal) technical assets of the CW-intelligence capacities of other states parties	
To prevent abuse of proscribed CW capabilities during the transition period preceding completion of their elimination under the CWC, but without impugning the Geneva Protocol	2 Procedure for safeguarding stocks of chemical weapons and production facilities for them prior to their elimination	4 Obligation to accept Procedure 2, the rule specifying the safeguards 5 Obligation to follow specified guidelines standardizing the rate and nature of national elimination processes	
To reduce ambiguities created by permitted retention of antichemical protection	3 Procedure for pooling information about activities permitted for protective purposes that are confusible with proscribed activities	6 Obligation to declare the information that will promote Procedure 3, the rule specifying inclusion of data on production and consumption of CW agents and the location of production capacity for especially threatening ones	'CW agents' (to include candidate agents) 'Especially threatening'
To reduce the likelihood of abuse of permitted retention of antichemical protection	4 Procedure for verifying compliance with Rule 7--i.e., ascertaining that production capacity for especially threatening CW agents is not being utilized beyond the agreed level	7 Ban on production of especially threatening CW agents beyond an agreed level (e.g., 0.1 ton/yr) 8 Obligation to accept Procedure 4. See, further, Rule 15 below	'Especially threatening CW agents'
To provide a mechanism whereby states parties remain free to retain all CW capability until such time as a significant number have committed themselves to the CWC	5 Procedure for mutual notification of duly ratified accessions to the CWC	9 Obligation to start implementing the provisions of the CWC as soon as a specified number of states, perhaps including particular states, have become parties	
he capability-elimination provisions: -- To enable states parties to demonstrate to others their elimination of proscribed capabilities in such a way as to promote assurance	6 Procedure for pooling information about states parties' plans for eliminating their now-proscribed capabilities, including progress reports on implementation and any revision of the plans 7 Procedure for the international display of the elimination of particular elements of proscribed CW capability, including stockpiles and production plant	10 Obligation to declare information enabling Procedure 6, the rule setting guidelines for the content of the initial declaration and follow-on ones 11 Obligation to eliminate stockpiles and production facilities within a specified period 12 Obligation to accept Procedure 7, the rule including an obligation to admit foreign observers to the sites of specified capability-elimination activities	'Production facilities'
-- To lengthen the lag-time between a decision to acquire proscribed CW capability and its actual acquisition	8 Procedure for verifying compliance with the Rule-1 ban on production of chemical weapons in its application to specified categories of toxic agent beyond permitted levels	13 Obligation to accept Procedure 8, the rule specifying the categories of toxic agent to be subject to such nonproduction verification, as well as the agreed procedures themselves	'Toxic agent' in differentiated categories
-- To enhance national CW-intelligence capacities by removing areas of ambiguity	9 Procedure for verifying compliance with Rule 14--i.e., ascertaining that production capacity for particularly ambivalent chemicals is not being utilized beyond the agreed level	14 Ban on production beyond an agreed level of particularly ambivalent chemicals that are not CW agents but whose production would involve activities especially easily confusible with proscribed activities 15 Obligation to accept Procedure 9, the rule, in its specification of the agreed permitted-production-verification procedure, being integrated with Rule 8 above	'Particularly ambivalent' 'Chemicals'

Provision for assuring CWC value, defined by function	Requisite international procedure	Requisite rule	Requisite definitions
The information provisions: — To enhance national CW-intelligence capacities by increasing access to hitherto secure data	10 Procedure for pooling information about prior activities now proscribed 11 Procedure for verifying information declared under Rule 16--i.e., for verifying some or all of the information pooled by Procedure 10 12 Procedure for verifying compliance with Rule 16--i.e., for ascertaining the absence of undeclared stockpiles and facilities	16 Obligation to declare information enabling Procedure 10, the rule specifying inclusion of data on current stockpiles (size, composition, location) and production facilities (capacity, products, location) 17 Obligation to accept Procedure 11, the rule specifying the agreed information-verification procedures 18 Obligation to accept Procedure 12, the rule specifying the agreed compliance-verification procedures	"Production facilities"
— To enhance national CW-intelligence capacities by making them better able to resolve ambiguities	13 Procedure for pooling information about permitted activities that are confusible with proscribed ones 14 Procedure for verifying information declared under Rule 19--i.e., for verifying some of the information pooled by Procedure 13	19 Obligation to declare information promoting Procedure 13, the rule specifying inclusion of data on production and consumption of major dual-purpose chemicals, such data to be declared regularly 20 Obligation to accept Procedure 14, the rule specifying the agreed information-verification procedures	"Major dual-purpose chemicals"
— To increase the likelihood of all information pooled by states parties reaching all relevant agencies of government	15 Procedure for pooling information about national organs charged with overseeing domestic implementation of the CWC	21 Obligation to establish adequately representative national implementation organs, the rule providing guidelines for their relationship to the Consultative Committee, and requiring information about their structure, duties and authority to be declared	
— To increase the probability of adequate pooling of information through safeguards reducing the possibilities for abuse of declared information	16 Procedure for controlling access to pooled information		
— To enable states parties to make nonobligatory disclosures of assuring information for confidence-building purposes	17 Procedure for facilitating non-obligatory disclosures of information (as by establishing a conducive Consultative Committee framework)		
The fall-back provisions: — Modernization provisions, for ensuring that all other provisions keep due pace with technical change	18 Procedure for pooling information about scientific and technical developments pertinent to CW (as by a conducive Consultative Committee framework) 19 Procedure for arriving at collective decisions about proposed amendments to the CWC	22 Obligation to participate in periodic reviews of scientific and technical developments pertinent to CW 23 Obligation to accept Procedure 19, the rule specifying the amendment procedure	
— Challenge provisions, for resolving serious suspicions of noncompliance and for protecting the regime against frivolous, scurrilous or ill-considered allegations of noncompliance	20 Procedure for the submission of information suggestive of noncompliance 21 Procedure for the submission of information responsive to complaints under Procedure 20 22 Procedure for arriving at a collective decision on a proposal for the fact-finding investigation of a complaint that has been subject to Procedures 20 and 21 23 Procedure for fact-finding in the event of a collective decision under Procedure 22 to investigate a complaint 24 Procedure for pooling information resulting from the fact-finding investigation of a complaint in accordance with Procedure 23	24 Obligation to accept Procedure 20 when publicizing suspicions of noncompliance, the rule requiring that prima facie evidence be included in the information submitted 25 Obligation to accept Procedure 21 as specified in this rule when responding to a complaint under Procedure 20 26 Obligation to accept Procedure 22, the rule specifying the decision-making procedure 27 Obligation to accept Procedure 23, the rule specifying the fact-finding procedure	
— Withdrawal provisions, for enabling states parties to withdraw from the regime without necessarily destroying it thereby	25 Procedure for mutual notification of duly noticed withdrawals from the CWC in accordance with Rule 28	28 Obligation to remain bound by the CWC unless extraordinary circumstances necessitate withdrawal, in which case an agreed period of prior notice must be given, together with an explanation of the circumstances	
— Mutual-assistance provisions, for ameliorating the most extreme consequences of inadequate assurance of compliance		29 Obligation to provide practical assistance to states parties victims of CW attack	

Chapter 7. The analytical framework completed

The synopsis presented in table 4 has 29 examples of the rules, and 25 of the procedures, that might be needed to give form to the assurance provisions. Those procedures include several that may be labelled 'verification procedures':

-- declared-information verification,

-- stockpile-destruction verification,

-- facility-elimination verification,

-- permitted-production verification,

-- nonproduction verification, and

-- nonretention verification.

There is, of course, nothing sacrosanct about any of the examples given: others might just as well have been included or substituted for the ones given. The purpose was simply to convey an overall impression of the necessary structure and content of the CWC, in particular the way in which certain sets of procedures and rules might be linked to one another in order to satisfy the requirement for adequate assurance in the most economical manner.

It is in such linkages that the device exists for adjusting the CWC-provisions to suit the needs of all the governments participating in the negotiations--assuming, that is, they are in fact striving for consensus. The needs will, as we have seen, vary widely and for widely differing reasons. Apart from anything else, the CWC will for some governments be a disarmament treaty, in which case its provisions for implementing capability-elimination without thereby endangering security will be of primary concern. For other governments, the great majority of those participating, the CWC will be a nonarmament treaty, in which case its provisions for assuring preclusion of future CW capability may appear more important. For accommodating such a wide span of needs, as well as the widely varying play of domestic interests, some of the linkages offer much more scope for adjustment than others without the assurance functions of the linked provisions being destroyed. In the sense of the overall framework of analysis which we are constructing, it is these particular linkages which have the greatest potential for matching the value of the international-collaboration basket to that of the national self-reliance basket.

The major options for adjusting the rules and procedures

Crucial to that bargain is, we have seen, the degree of assurance of CWC-compliance that is on offer. In essence, the assurance strategy which we have been developing for our analytical framework is one that deliberately exploits a permitted retention of two elements of national self-reliance: CW-intelligence capacity and antichemical protection. The more that governments can look to their own intelligence machinery for assurance of CWC-compliance on the part of potential enemies, the less will they require from the CWC the provision of special international machinery for providing assurance by verifying this or that aspect of compliance. Here, then, is one of the major linkages. It connects at one end the rules and procedures for instituting and operating that special machinery in its various conceivable forms to, at the other end, those rules and procedures whose effect is to enhance national CW-intelligence capacity--the devices for, in effect, increasing the transparency of the military-industrial milieu within which proscribed activities would, if they were happening, be being conducted. Such devices chiefly comprise the various information-pooling procedures, based on obligatory declarations, exemplified in table 4; they also include the device of verified bans on particularly ambiguous activities. And they necessarily include the devices for restoring some of the transparency destroyed by the permitted retention of antichemical protection.

The reason why the trade-off possibilities inherent in this particular linkage are so great stems from the nature of the special international machinery. If the national intelligence machinery at the opposite end of the linkage were capable of providing a substantial degree of assurance, the country possessing it, and others having access to it, might be able to look to the international machinery for little more than confirmatory or confidence-building information, or as a means for disseminating such of its own intelligence as it chose to release. But if the national machinery were weak, information of a much harder and more extensive kind might be sought from the international machinery, information which might be forthcoming only if the international machinery intruded deeply into the domestic affairs of states parties, for example by frequent on-site inspections or by close scrutiny of the books of individual industrial enterprises. Such intrusions could require, for their acceptance in the first place, substantial sacrifices on the part of domestic interests, and tolerance of major encroachments upon national sovereignty. Better, then, it might be thought, for governments to accept the more limited derogations from their sovereignty implicit in rules requiring them to declare information, rather than the more serious derogations resulting from their being required to admit foreign agencies into their domains in quest of much the same information.

The problem with this particular form of trade-off is that it creates a new area of uncertainty, thereby, at least in theory, creating new assurance requirements: how confident can states parties be that their potential enemies have not falsified their declarations? One remedy--envisaged in table 4--is to institute international machinery for verifying the information declared: for ascertaining, for instance, that such and such a factory really is producing only the pesticides declared for it, or that that storage building really does only contain 10 000 medium-calibre artillery shell charged with mustard gas. But that is only a partial remedy. In the case of nonproduction verification, it might perhaps be a sufficient one, nevertheless, for production on any scale, however secret, necessarily represents a continual expenditure of resources; it is possible that any such expenditure on a significant scale could be tracked and characterized by what has been called 'second-order' verification processes [23] conducted by either national or international agencies. Even in the case of stockpile-destruction verification, it would not necessarily be a totally inadequate remedy. Stockpiles are more easily concealed than agent factories, but they are still in a sense living things, requiring sustenance if they are to constitute part of a viable military capability; undeclared stockpiles, too, could manifest themselves to second-order verification.

Most likely, there is no full remedy: declarations procedures for verifying compliance, however well supported they may be by international arrangements for verifying the information declared and by second-order techniques, will always leave loopholes for cheaters or perceivers of cheating. Most likely, also, there is no alternative. Verification of compliance with a negative obligation--such as a ban on stockpiling of chemical weapons--is the proving of a negative. It is therefore, very probably, no more feasible than gaining assurance that declarations were what they should have been--even if a whole army of inspectors were to tour all countries, and even if all states parties extended permanently open invitations for such inspection. Which, one may ask, could prove the more damaging for the CWC regime: the limited nature of the assurance available from declarations procedures incorporating information-verification arrangements, or the possibly false nature of the assurance derivable from compliance-verification arrangements under the charge of an international inspectorate? Some of both approaches would seem to be what is needed: an intermediate setting of this particular linkage.

A second major linkage offering a broad range of adjustment options is the one that connects the various fallback provisions to the capability-elimination and information provisions. The smaller the assurance derivable from the CWC's routine procedures, the greater is the load placed on the fallback provisions, above all the challenge procedures. So much so, in fact, that special international machinery comprising little more than well-developed challenge provisions might be deemed acceptable by some states parties, especially those with well-endowed national machinery. A limit to this second form of trade-off possibility is, however, set by the extent to which governments are prepared to commit themselves in advance under the challenge provisions to admitting into their territory fact-finding investigators charged with the task of gathering information that might--correctly or erroneously--incriminate them. The less inclined the negotiating partners are to accept the principle of mandatory challenge inspection, the more reliance must be placed on the routine international machinery, and therefore the more accommodating must it be.

Finally, we should note here, once again, the adjustment options available in the range of alternatives for the precise structure, mandate and relationship with national implementation organs of the Consultative Committee. Even small changes in whatever may be proposed could, because of the critical role which the Committee will have in mediating the CWC procedures, have a major influence on the degree of assurance derivable from them. And we should recall, too, the still more fundamental adjustment options available in, first, the manner in which 'chemical weapons' and 'permitted purposes' are to be defined, and, secondly, in the concordance of threat-level and control-level.

Completing the analytical framework

From these considerations, the final structure of our overall framework of analysis may be completed. The last conceptual building-block to be fitted in is this. For any one government, the breakeven point at which international collaboration in the CWC may be judged no less beneficial to the national security than existing measures of national self-reliance may be approached by seeking the acceptance of other governments for that particular balance between the challenge provisions of the CWC, its routine international implementation machinery, and its devices for enhancing national CW-intelligence capacity that that government has found to be acceptable to its dominant domestic interests. If such a balance cannot be found, the government must attempt to impose one. The linkages between those three categories of treaty provision are, we may now see, adjustable to provide much scope for minimizing sacrifices without losing security benefit. And by the same token they allow substantial latitude for intergovernmental accommodations, no less than for domestic ones.

So we may now list those particular topics for intergovernmental negotiation on the outcome of which principally depends the viability of the arms-control route to security against the CW threat:

1. The definitions whose effect it will be to establish the concordance between the degree of threat that particular chemicals represent to the national security and the degree of control to which they will be subject under the CWC regime.

2. The extent to which the information which states need to assure themselves of adversary compliance is to be derived from special international machinery established for the purpose, as opposed to being furnished or gathered by states parties themselves.

3. The extent to which that special international machinery is to operate on a routine basis, as opposed to its being activated only upon challenges of suspected noncompliance.

4. The extent to which states parties are prepared to delegate authority to whatever organization they agree to establish to oversee implementation of the CWC.

Should intergovernmental consensus on these four key matters not be available, then the options for future CW policy-making would recede towards measures of national self-reliance only.

Applying the analytical framework

Our objective in constructing the analytical framework has been more than to provide a convenient scheme for relating to one another the different factors that go into policy-making for CW-preparedness or CW-threat-mitigation. We have been aiming for prescriptive as well as descriptive value. How the framework might best be applied in developing actual recommendations for policy or a particular set of proposals for the content of a CWC draft is to be the subject of later study. But some preliminary observations need making here by way of conclusion.

Some countervailing principles

First, a caveat must be entered. As a tool for assessing competing negotiating options, the framework is biased against the interests of politically weak groups. The fact that their political influence is weak does not necessarily mean that principles in which their interests find expression are irrelevant to security and therefore to the purpose of the CWC. In some cases they are patently of high relevance, but are liable to be ignored simply because the relevance is for the medium or long term. There is an inevitable tendency in government, which is necessarily preoccupied with its immediate press of business, for subordinating what is best for the long term to what is convenient for the short term. Our analytical framework therefore has prescriptive merit only if it is applied in express conjunction with certain principles that might otherwise fall foul of short-term expediency.

These countervailing principles exist in both positive and negative forms: principles requiring the presence of particular types of provision in the CWC, and principles requiring the absence of other types of provision. The following, briefly stated, are examples.

The CWC must be nondiscriminatory. The regime will depend on the mutual confidence that stems from its collaborative undertakings. If there is discrimination in any important sense, the collaboration will be weakened and confidence liable to fade. At least four discriminatory tendencies can be discerned in the Geneva negotiations: against states in a condition of underdevelopment; against states not at present possessing chemical weapons; against states uninvolved, or weakly involved, in the present European military confrontation; and against states whose military-industrial milieux are relatively transparent to external gaze.

<u>The CWC must not interfere with industrial development</u>. This principle has often found expression in Geneva and is included in this listing primarily for that reason. In the sense that industrial interests should be accorded a special respect in the design of controls, the principle is hardly likely to escape application in the counsels of the industrialized nations, and is fully embodied in the framework. In the alternative sense of respect for the development goals of the less industrialized nations, it is a restatement of the foregoing principle.

<u>The mechanisms for assuring compliance must be robust</u>. If the CWC does not provide mechanisms for restoring confidence in it that particular events might erode, its mechanisms for creating that confidence in the first place may be futile. Present attitudes towards the Biological Weapons Convention, in the aftermath of the Sverdlovsk anthrax and 'yellow rain' episodes, illustrate this principle. The CWC assurance provisions must be able to withstand moments of at least moderate stress. This is a principle that might find its best expression in a conscious development of linkages between the confidence-building, information and challenge provisions.

<u>The CWC must not erode the existing anti-CBW regime</u>. In endeavouring to build upon and extend the present regime of CBW constraints, the CWC must avoid provisions whose effect may actually be to weaken that regime.

<u>The CWC must be counter-assimilatory</u>. If the CWC does not provide strong obstacles to the process of assimilation of chemical weapons, it will, for the reasons described in chapter 4, be short-lived. It may therefore be important to consider ways and means for bringing the research and development components of chemical-weapons capability under some degree of formal constraint; likewise its doctrinal and

organizational components. Special care must be taken to constrain possible abuses of the permitted antichemical protective activities. Such controls could ultimately prove to be among the most important elements of the CWC regime.

Regardless of our analytical framework, these are all principles which require more than lip-service in Geneva, above all because there it is a fact of life that the negotiations are paced very largely by the behaviour of the USA and the USSR. The superpowers have set not only the rate of progress, but also its direction. This we may see in the disproportionate attention which the CD has given to the problems of capability-elimination as compared with problems of capability-preclusion, the appearance thereby being created that the principal security-danger which the CWC must guard against is that of the CW-disarmament process itself rather than that of chemical-weapons proliferation, for example, or of the utility of chemical weapons in North-South conflict. And because those CW-disarmament dangers are thought of chiefly in the context of the primary superpower confrontation--in Europe--rather than, for example, in a context such as that of the Gulf War, the negotiations have long been displaying a conspicuously Eurocentric bias.

Matters for further inquiry

In order to construct our framework, we have been obliged to examine ways in which the value, in security terms, of international collaboration under this or that conceivable CWC regime might be assured. We chose to rely upon a warning-time conception. Such an approach admitted into the framework a device for assessing the security value of competing CWC options in addition to its basic function of showing how those options might be constructed in such a way that they would have any sort of security value at all.

We did not, however, dwell in any comparable detail upon ways for assessing the security value of the alternatives to international collaboration, namely national measures of self-reliance. In this respect, therefore, our framework is lopsided. Were it the case that the available literature addressed the topic adequately, the imbalance would not impede application of our framework. But in fact the security significance of chemical weapons is a subject that has largely been neglected by those defence and security analysts who work in the open domain; and those studies that are available in non-secret form are almost all concerned with the value of chemical weapons to particular countries. What is lacking is what we need most: a comparative analysis of the value of the weapons to different types of country.

To a degree which may almost be sufficient, this subject can be addressed in general terms. Given the existence of the current Geneva-Protocol-based anti-CW regime, it is not in theory necessary to examine the security significance of chemical weapons except insofar as their retaliatory utility is concerned. In that case the primary consideration becomes the matter which we have touched upon in various parts of chapter 4: do chemical weapons have a real propensity for deterring resort to chemical warfare and, if so, how important might such deterrence be for the security of different countries? One consequence of the superpower domination, just referred to, of the Geneva negotiations is that belief in the like-with-like deterrence value of chemical weapons has spread in recent years. It is obviously of central importance for the future of the negotiations that this belief be subjected to a far more rigorous scrutiny than it so far appears, from the open literature, to have received. Should it transpire that the belief is well founded, then the process of CW-disarmament might indeed introduce new dangers into the world, albeit ones that should easily be containable by appropriate assurance provisions. Should the opposite conclusion be reached, it would follow that the real security value of the national self-reliance option to be renounced under the CWC would be so slight as to be easily outweighed by that of a very modest CWC. The value of the treaty would then be governed by the strength of the constraint that it placed on any further assimilation and proliferation of chemical weapons.

CW deterrence is not, however, a topic that lends itself at all readily to objective analysis. Conclusions one way or the other can be reached easily enough, but only from subjective premises. An illustration of such an analysis is given in the annex.

There is a further, quite different, topic which also requires more study than it has yet received. In the barter model on which our framework is based, as in the Geneva negotiations themselves, the principal actors are governments. The presumption is, accordingly, that all the factors that are relevant to the creation and operation of the CWC regime are sufficiently controllable by governments. This may indeed be so; but it is as well to recognize that an increasing proportion of the dealings between countries nowadays is not mediated through governments. Most governments have retained to themselves instruments of control, which some use more rigorously than others. Yet it is not impossible to envisage CWC-related dealings for which the instruments may be inadequate. There are two areas in particular where such possibilities arise. One is the case of transnational corporations active in chemical manufacturing industry. Another exists in the commodious networks of communication which the world's scientific community has developed for itself, and on which it depends heavily for its well-being.

The question which is really being raised here is whether the Geneva negotiators (and our analytical framework) are adequately representative of all the interests on whose goodwill and co-operation the CWC regime will depend. If there is not a problem of governmental control, there could still be one of communication--communication both in the sense of adequate channels existing for the purpose and in the sense of comprehension of what passes through those channels. It is evident from the Geneva talks that not all of the governments or governmental agencies represented there are in full and sufficient communication with industrial and scientific interests. The matter for further study, then, is the nature of the mechanisms for achieving fuller communication, especially while the CWC is still being negotiated: mechanisms perhaps involving international nongovernmental organizations.

References

1. Meselson, M.S. (editor). Chemical Weapons and Chemical Arms Control. Washington, D.C.: Carnegie Endowment, 1978.

2. Bulgaria, Czechoslovakia, Hungary, Mongolia, Poland, Romania and the USSR. Conference of the Committee on Disarmament document CCD/361 of 28 March 1972.

3. Argentina, Brazil, Burma, Egypt, Ethiopia, Mexico, Morocco, Nigeria, Sweden and Yugoslavia. Conference of the Committee on Disarmament document CCD/400* of 26 April 1973.

4. Japan. Conference of the Committee on Disarmament document CCD/420 of 30 April 1974, and document CCD/452 of 8 April 1975.

5. United Kingdom. Conference of the Committee on Disarmament document CCD/512 of 6 August 1976.

6. United States. Conference on Disarmament document CD/500 of 18 April 1984.

7. USA and USSR. Committee on Disarmament document CD/112 of 7 July 1980.

8. Robinson, J.P.P. 'Chemical arms control and the assimilation of chemical weapons'. International Journal (Toronto), Vol. 36, No. 3 (Summer 1981), pp. 515-34.

9. Robinson, J.P.P. 'Chemical, biological and radiological warfare: futures from the past'. Submission to the Independent Commission on Disarmament and Security Issues (Chairman: O. Palme), September 1981.

10. Haas, E. 'Why collaborate? Issue linkage and international regimes'. World Politics, Vol. 32 (April 1980), pp. 357-405.

11. Schiff, B.N. International Nuclear Technology Transfer. Totowa, New Jersey: Rowman & Allenheld, and London: Croom Helm, 1984.

12. USSR. Committee on Disarmament document CD/294 of 21 July 1982.

13. Independent Commission on Disarmament and Security Issues (Chairman: O. Palme). Common Security: A Programme for Disarmament. London: Pan, 1982.

14. SIPRI. Policies for Common Security. London: Taylor & Francis, 1985.

15. Hedén, C.-G. In SIPRI, The Problem of Chemical and Biological Warfare, Vol. 2. Stockholm: Almqvist & Wiksell, 1973, pp. 19-21.

16. Trumpener, U. 'The road to Ypres: the beginnings of gas warfare in World War I'. Journal of Modern History, Vol. 47 (September 1975), pp. 460-480.

17. Hewitt, S.G. 'Aspects of the social history of chemical warfare in World War One'. M Sc dissertation, University of Sussex, England, August 1972.

18. Neild, R.R. In SIPRI, The Problem of Chemical and Biological Warfare, Vol. 5. Stockholm: Almqvist & Wiksell, 1971, p. 98.

19. Brown, F.J. 'United States chemical warfare policy, 1919-1945'. Doctoral dissertation (thesis no. 174), University of Geneva, May 1966. This was the basis for his Chemical Warfare: A Study in Restraints. Princeton: Princeton University Press, 1968.

20. This idea was suggested in a personal communication from B. ter Haar and A.J. Meerburg, December 1984.

21. In relation to the CWC, it is useful to distance the concepts of 'verifiability' and 'verification'; see further, Robinson, J.P.P., 'CW verification: a reappraisal in the light of the recent past', a paper presented at the 3rd Workshop of the Pugwash CW Study Group, London, April 1976; and 'Should NATO keep chemical weapons? A framework for considering policy alternatives', SPRU Occasional Paper Series (University of Sussex: Science Policy Research Unit), No. 4, August 1977; and 'The negotiations on chemical-warfare arms control', Arms Control, Vol. 1, No. 1 (May 1980), pp. 30-52.

22. Lundin, S.J. 'Considerations on a chemical arms control treaty and the concept of amplified verification'. FOA Reports (Sweden National Defence Research Institute), Vol. 7, No. 1, 1973.

23. Concepts of second-order verification, and the initial studies of its potential application, are to be found in the seminal work on CBW arms control by A.R. Pittaway, extended by R.E. Roberts, during the late 1960s. Regrettably, most of this work is unavailable in the open literature; see, however: (a) Pittaway, A.R. Prepared statement before the Subcommittee on National Security Policy and Scientific Developments of the Committee on Foreign Affairs, US House of Representatives, during a hearing on 2 May 1974 (Hearings, U.S. Chemical Warfare Policy, pp. 76-90); and (b) Roberts, R.E. and Cunningham, C.L. 'Economic monitoring of arms control agreements--chemical warfare agents', a contract report (No. ACDA/E-183) from the Midwest Research Institute to the US Arms Control & Disarmament Agency, 21 April 1971.

Annex. The value of chemical weapons for deterrence

It is from deterrence theory that the broad rationales for possessing chemical weapons have long been derived. Governments are prevented from displaying in public any other rationales, for the 1925 Geneva Protocol requires that resort to the weapons be contemplated only for reprisal or in-kind retaliation.

Enunciation of deterrence rationales predates the Geneva Protocol, however. They first emerged during the immediate aftermath of World War I, in what has remained their most ambitious form. A strong CW capability could, it was claimed by the Chief of the US Army Chemical Warfare Service in his annual report for 1920, "go a long way toward deterring [other countries] from forcing hostilities". This was in keeping with the widespread reaction to what a few years earlier had been the first concerted appearance of science on the battlefield. It was, for example, the considered view of the US Navy in 1921 that "Gas warfare threatens to become so efficient as to endanger the very existence of civilization". Nuclear weapons have since obscured poison gas in such perceptions, but belief in the general war deterring propensity of CW armament still survives. It does so in two forms.

One is in the idea that non-nuclear-weapon states might see chemical (or biological) weapons as accessible alternatives to nuclear weapons--the 'poor man's deterrent'. In fact the idea rarely seems to have much currency in those parts of the world where its proponents deem it applicable. The regions from which there are occasional rumours of interest are all ones into which the proliferation of nuclear weapons has been thought imminent.

The second form, relating to nuclear-weapon states, is contained in the following proposition. If deterrence of aggression is to succeed, it must be rooted in the maintenance of a range of retaliatory and other military options that is patently capable of countering attack at whatever level it is delivered; any gap in that range might, because of mutual deterrence existing at higher escalatory levels, constitute a 'window of opportunity' for an aggressor, thus vitiating the entire deterrent posture. It is this notion of an imbalance in the chemical armament of opposing forces amounting to a gap having what would in effect be strategic significance that provides the most influential rationale today for maintaining chemical-weapons capabilities.

Yet in fact most of the public debate about CW deterrence is couched in rather less subtle terms. As the headline of a Western newspaper editorial calling for CW rearmament put it recently, 'Gas Deters Gas': a simple expression of faith which does not require its adherents to think too closely about how in-kind CW deterrence is supposed to operate, and not at all about how it might contribute to the general deterrence of war. As in that example, it is a common feature of most writing on CW today for the subject to be considered in isolation from its background of other forms of military capability, conventional as well as nuclear--as though CW were somehow outside the context of those overall war-fighting and war-deterring doctrines which provide the rationale for all forms of military capability. Such simplification naturally encourages simplistic thinking, as in this very common proposition: If we have no chemical weapons with which to retaliate against CW attack, we shall be forced to use nuclear weapons.

The 'window of opportunity' conception imputes to chemical weapons an ability to function as an intra-war deterrent of CW. One way of analysing its plausibility is to identify the prerequisites which the conception must satisfy if the intra-war deterrence is to operate.

To believe in the necessity for a special intra-war deterrent is tantamount to believing that without it the general deterrent would be ineffective. To believe that for

CW retaliatory capability is in turn to believe that at least three preconditions obtain, as follows.

One precondition is that opposing nuclear forces really have deterred themselves out of all practical relevance to actual war-fighting: circumstances, in other words, in which a belligerent could feel confident that his resort to chemical weapons in otherwise conventional warfare carried a negligible risk of inciting nuclear retaliation. Given the magnitude of the constraints that are likely to inhibit nuclear release, this is a precondition that might well be satisfied in fighting that had not yet progressed at all far up the scale of conceivable intensity, or in which the discernible war-aims were apparently modest ones.

The second precondition is that the chemical forces available to the potential initiator of CW--call her country A--were of such great tactical utility that, only by using them in conjunction with her conventional forces, could A be confident of achieving her war-aims. Whether this precondition can be satisfied depends on the nature both of those chemical forces and of the antichemical protection of country B's defending forces arrayed against them.

There is an alternative version of the second precondition, namely that the tactical predicament of A has become so dire that unless she uses all the forces at her immediate disposal, including her chemical forces, she faces defeat at worst or nonattainment of her original war-aims at best. In this rendering, satisfaction of the precondition depends entirely on the antichemical protectedness of B's forces--on its ability, or lack thereof, to allow those forces to prevail.

The third precondition is that B's retaliatory use of chemical weapons could offer such an increase in the effectiveness of B's operations as to deny A her war-aims. Whether this precondition can be satisfied depends on the nature of B's chemical forces and A's antichemical protection.

Since the time of World War II, measures of protection against CW attack have improved greatly in efficacy, so much so that, when properly exploited, they are capable of diminishing the potential mass-destructiveness of CW attacks to the point where major tactical gains can be expected only if the defence is taken by surprise, before protection can be fully assumed. Retaliation in kind would confront a fully alerted antichemical stance, meaning that the damage it threatened could be trivial in comparison with that of a surprise initiatory attack. This suggests that the prospects for satisfying the third precondition would never be great. That at least would seem to be the conclusion if the matter is considered in terms of this generality.

Yet in more specific or scenario-based terms the conclusion could be different, especially if chemical forces are seen as an element, not of firepower, but of manoeuvre. Let us therefore look specifically at the present NATO/WTO confrontation in Europe.

The US Defense Department in on the public record as believing that its forces in Europe are now well enough protected to be capable of surviving any surprise CW attack that Soviet/WTO forces might deliver. Soviet forces in Europe are believed by an authoritative British analyst to be less capable of surviving surprise CW attack but more capable of withstanding anticipated or repeated ones. If all that is indeed so, it would seem that chemical forces would have value to NATO against Soviet forces, not as an intra-war CW deterrent (for that would fall foul of the third precondition), but as first-use weapons. And they would have value to WTO against US forces, not as a first-use weapon (for that would fall foul of the second precondition), but as a CW deterrent.

But the question then arises as to what the impact on the effectiveness of opposing forces might be, not of chemical weapons, but of the antichemical protective countermeasures that they call forth. There is no doubt that, with today's technology, antichemical protection is an encumbrance and likely to be degradative of combat efficiency. Given the technological differences on either side of the European confrontation, might the degradation imposed be significantly asymmetric, even to the point where the second and third preconditions obtain?

Two broad ways may be conceived in which chemical forces might be structured so that their use in retaliation would maximize the degradative impact of the antichemical protective posture they enforce.

The first would be based on the presumption that the enemy would attach vital importance to maintaining the tempo and momentum of any assault in which he had gone to the extreme of resorting to chemical warfare. The more encumbering his antichemical protection and the more time-demanding his decontamination procedures, the more gravely might both tempo and forward momentum be affected. The fact that enemy units would in any case have had to assume some level of antichemical protection against the collateral effects of their own initiatory CW operations--a protective posture duly orientated towards their particular combat missions--would of course have to enter into any reckoning of the overall impact of the retaliation in kind. The retaliatory capability needed would have to be one that was widely dispersed among the defending forces and usable very rapidly. This would require forward defence units to carry chemical munitions as part of their basic tactical load, and to be well indoctrinated in their use. It would also require delegation of release authority to levels rather low in the military command structure.

The second route to maximization would involve a capability for executing selective attacks on rear-area targets chosen both for the importance of their mission to enemy operations or strategy and for the vulnerability of those missions to the delays and other difficulties stemming from the necessity of decontamination. Deep-strike targets of this type might include tactical airfields or logistical centres (as at harbours, railway complexes or, again, airfields). The requirement would be for long-range weapons capable of dispensing persistent CW agents over wide areas: strike aircraft or theatre-range guided missiles.

Two broad points may be made about this pair of options. The first is that the capabilities providing those options could as well be exploited for initiatory as for retaliatory use; which is to say they might serve both the second and the third preconditions for both sides. In that event, any in-kind deterrence that the new capabilities established would also--on the assumption that both sides acquired them--have aggravated, even induced, the threat they were supposed to be deterring. The second point is that the rate of technical change in the field of antichemical protection is currently in a growth phase. Among the new equipments that are being fielded, or soon will be, are less encumbering respirators and gloves, less heat-stressful protective clothing, scanning field alarms, more efficient decontaminants and applicators for them, and so on. Survivability and maintainability within a CW-contaminated environment are becoming basic design requirements for all types of military equipment. Therefore, the 'window of opportunity', if indeed it exists, is being narrowed by antichemical protective technology. Nor is that technology alone, alongside chemical-weapons technology, in offering a narrowing of the window. While CW agents may indeed have target effects or other properties which make them capable of providing the two forms of tactical-offset/deterrence just outlined, there is an expanding range of conventional munitions that have the same capability. For example, special value has been seen in the use of persistent CW agents against tactical airfields for degrading the enemy sortie-rate. But for that counter-air role, the new varieties of conventional airfield-attack submunition weapons may be competitive in cost-effectiveness terms. Similar examples can be found for most, and probably all, the other operational roles envisaged for chemical weapons, whether in forward defence, close air support, battlefield interdiction or deep interdiction.

This last consideration is especially pertinent to the postulated deep-strike route to in-kind CW deterrence, for there are other reasons why conventional, not chemical, attack could serve the operational ends sought (interdiction) from the retaliation more effectively. Above all, there would be substantial difficulties in imparting sufficient credibility to the threat of long-range chemical attack for it to provide actual deterrence. The execution of this threat would inevitably afflict large numbers of unprotected noncombatants. The possibility of such mass-destructiveness would carry with it the possibility, maybe the likelihood, of mass-destructive counter-attack, in which case the CW deep-strike route might either be self-deterring or self-defeating. Escalation-control would be weakened. So it might for the other postulated route to in-kind CW deterrence, namely threatened exploitation of a forward-deployed quick-response retaliatory capability. To achieve such a capability would necessarily involve diminished command-and-control of the retaliatory weapons, with the risk of the retaliatory forces actually being used to initiate CW, whether through inadvertence or through the impetuousness of one of the, say, battalion commanders to whom release authority would have had to have been delegated.

Let us, even so, ignore all these objections, and look from another angle at the options for maximizing the degradative impact of enforced antichemical precautions. The two main ones which we have been considering derive whatever propensity they have for in-kind deterrence first from postural differences existing between the forces of the initiator and those of the retaliator, forward or rear, and secondly from the chances of the retaliatory capability exploiting those differences at moments of maximal vulnerability. The opportunities for such exploitation would be strongly contingent upon the precise course of battlefield events theatre-wide.

We can thus see that there is actually a fourth precondition over and above those we have already identified: that the retaliatory capability be so closely integrated into the forces and doctrines of its possessor, and its release procedures so well prepared, that it can be used without significant delay, before such opportunities pass.

For a category of weapon whose use is illegal, this is a most difficult precondition for any armed service to meet, for the lower the expectation of a particular weapon being ordered into use, the lower will be the incentive acting upon the relevant training, doctrine-development and logistics commands to assimilate the weapon--to give it the requisite priority over other pressing duties. Nor is it likely that the political leadership of the country will be at all eager to delegate release authority to levels from which field commanders could receive it without significant delay. A contradiction is thus generated. Unintegrated, the weapon may not deter, in which case the expectation of non-use that impedes integration may prove inaccurate; but, integrated, it may deter, thereby validating the expectation.

There are two ways out of this contradiction. Either ignore the international law which prohibits use of the weapon, abandoning the no-first-use policy which sustains the contradiction. Or abandon the weapons and rely, as against any other form of enemy attack, on the general capabilities and competences of the defence forces to counter whatever tactical gain an enemy might achieve with poison gas. Against good antichemical protection such gains may be no more than marginal or strongly localized.

For Product Safety Concerns and Information please contact our EU representative GPSR@taylorandfrancis.com
Taylor & Francis Verlag GmbH, Kaufingerstraße 24, 80331 München, Germany

www.ingramcontent.com/pod-product-compliance
Lightning Source LLC
Chambersburg PA
CBHW052132300426
44116CB00010B/1866
* 9 7 8 0 3 6 7 6 2 7 5 4 6 *